The Case for
Economic Democracy

T0048626

The Case For series

Sam Pizzigati, *The Case for a Maximum Wage*

Louise Haagh, *The Case for Universal
Basic Income*

James K. Boyce, *The Case for Carbon Dividends*

Frances Coppola, *The Case for People's
Quantitative Easing*

Joe Guinan & Martin O'Neill, *The Case for
Community Wealth Building*

Anna Coote & Andrew Percy, *The Case for
Universal Basic Services*

Gerald Friedman, *The Case for Medicare for All*

Andrew Cumbers, *The Case for Economic
Democracy*

Andrew Cumbers

The Case for Economic Democracy

polity

First published in 2020 by Polity Press

Polity Press
65 Bridge Street
Cambridge CB2 1UR, UK

Polity Press
101 Station Landing
Suite 300
Medford, MA 02155, USA

ISBN-13: 978-1-5095-3384-8
ISBN-13: 978-1-5095-3385-5 (pb)

A catalogue record for this book is available from the British Library.

Library of Congress Cataloging-in-Publication Data

Names: Cumbers, Andrew, author.
Title: The case for economic democracy / Andrew Cumbers.
Description: Cambridge, UK ; Medford, MA : Polity, 2020. | Series: The case
  for | Includes bibliographical references. | Summary: "Andrew Cumbers
  shows why economic democracy's time has come"-- Provided by publisher.
Identifiers: LCCN 2019034779 (print) | LCCN 2019034780 (ebook) | ISBN
  9781509533848 (hardback) | ISBN 9781509533855 (paperback) | ISBN
  9781509533862 (epub)
Subjects: LCSH: Distributive justice. | Social justice. | Democratization.
Classification: LCC HB523 .C84 2020 (print) | LCC HB523 (ebook) | DDC
  330.01--dc23
LC record available at https://lccn.loc.gov/2019034779
LC ebook record available at https://lccn.loc.gov/2019034780

Typeset in 11 on 15 Sabon by Servis Filmsetting Ltd, Stockport, Cheshire
Printed and bound in the UK by CPI Group (UK) Ltd, Croydon

For further information on Polity, visit our website: politybooks.com

Contents

Tables and Figures

Acknowledgements

I am grateful to the Adam Smith Business School and the wider academic community at the University of Glasgow for providing me with the space, time and collegiality to help me complete this book. Special thanks are due to Robert McMaster who has been my partner on the related project to construct an Economic Democracy Index, and who has been the source of important discussions and insights on economic democracy over almost two decades. I am grateful too to the ESRC for the initial funding for that project 'Transforming Public Policy through Economic Democracy' (REf: ES/N006674/1), which helped to develop some of the ideas behind this book. Our other co-investigators on that project, Michael White, Susana Cabaco and Karen Bilsland, also deserve thanks for their support in various ways over the past four years.

Acknowledgements

Special thanks are also due to David Featherstone for his broader insights on progressive and radical thought. Outside Glasgow, Thomas Hanna, Joe Guinan and Gar Alperovitz of the Democracy Collaborative, Andy Pike and Danny MacKinnon at CURDS, Geoff Whittam and Katherine Trebeck have all in different ways been a source of ideas, debate and creative thinking that have helped me clarify and refine my arguments over the past decade. Thanks also to George Owers, my editor (plus three anonymous referees) for the perceptive and insightful thoughts and comments that have greatly improved the book. All remaining errors are of course mine. Thanks also to George and Julia Davies at Polity for their patience and support through the numerous missed deadlines. Anni Pues has, as ever, been an ever-present source of love, encouragement and inspiration. Finally, thanks to Anna and David for their constant reminders that there is more to life than work.

Introduction

As we enter the third decade of the twenty-first century, the world is at a crossroads with a number of inter-related economic, ecological and political crises. Economically, there are widening inequalities between rich and poor, and a growing chasm between the elite billionaire class and the rest of us. Linked to this unequal and imbalanced system of global capitalism, we face an environmental catastrophe with global warming brought on by two centuries of rampant industrialization and ill-considered economic growth. Even if we can mitigate its worst effects, the rapid depletion of our natural resources in pursuit of profit threatens to leave the planet barely fit for habitation by future generations. Taken together, these economic and ecological crises are producing a third crisis, the focus of much public debate and angst among media, academic commentators and our ruling classes. This is the crisis of democracy itself.

When most people talk of democracy, they are almost certainly thinking about political democracy with a capital 'P': elections, representative government, political parties, the relations between parliament and the public. Very little consideration is given to whether the economy itself should also be thought of in democratic terms. Yet, how the economy functions, who controls it and makes key decisions regarding how it functions, what is produced and who benefits, is fundamental to everything else in our lives. Accessing the economic resources to lead decent lives, doing so in a way that is fair to others, and sustainable in caring for the planet and future generations, should surely be at the core of our discussions about democracy.

This book is motivated by the absence of these issues from public debate. In writing it, I aim to put the question of democratizing the economy back onto the agenda, making the case for economic democracy an important step in dealing with the manifold crises that we face. From the outset we should note that democracy – by any meaningful definition of the term – is absent both from the workplace and the wider economy. In the workplace, workers have diminishing rights over enterprise decision making, trade unions are in retreat and collective bargaining is under attack. There is still a tradition of cooperatives and employee-owned enterprises, nominally committed to democratic practice, though these are marginal to the dominant corporate and privatized economy. More broadly, whether we are talking about the big macroeconomic decisions, such as the setting of interest rates, fiscal decisions about how much tax and spending is required (apart from highly superficial election-time debates), or more fundamental questions over what forms of economic organization, ownership and institutions are required to combat the climate emergency, the broader public has little real say or participation in how the economy functions.

It is my view that the absence of democracy from the economy is a fundamental crisis in itself. A functioning democracy, in a stable and civilized society, is one that respects the rights of individuals, citizens and communities to participate on equal terms in the public and civic realms of that society. Given the central importance of the economy in providing the resources necessary for a society to flourish, the decision making around these resources should be a matter for public engagement and democratic debate.

From this departure point, my intention with this book is to make a renewed case for economic democracy appropriate for our times. To do this, I develop an expansive sense of economic democracy and how this might be applied in the twenty-first century. This involves addressing a set of issues around what concepts, institutions and political agency are required to enable us to move from a capitalist, largely privatized and marketized economy – driven by narrow self-interest and greed – towards a more democratic economy, capable of serving the common good in tackling the ever more prescient social and ecological crises that we face.

The economic roots of the democratic crisis

The re-emergence of an authoritarian, xenophobic and fundamentally anti-democratic right-wing politics, symbolized by Donald Trump's US Presidency, is one of the key features of our time. On every continent, the retreat from universal human rights, international solidarity, respect for minorities, a tolerance of migrants and refugees and a commitment to shared solutions to global problems is a disturbing reality. As I write (in July 2019), a striking fact is that none of the world's ten most populated countries, which includes 'nominal' democracies such as Brazil, Russia, India and the United States, is listed by the Economist Intelligence Unit (EIU) as a 'Full Democracy' in its 2018 Democracy Index, which measures among other things, the commitment to pluralism, civil liberties and political culture. The EIU has noted 'a broad-based deterioration in the practice of democracy in recent years' (EIU 2017: 3).

Among many liberal academic and political commentators, there seems general agreement on what the problem is: a growing chasm between global elites and an increasingly disaffected populace, in part characterized as a 'deepening divide between people and experts' as the EIU puts it. The rejection of the existing political system leads to support for faux 'outsiders' – those members of the economic elite, like Trump, who can successfully position themselves to appeal to underlying nationalist and racist tropes among key voter groups, especially those 'left behind' by economic globalization.

While the crisis of democracy is now a central trope of mainstream commentary, there is seldom much discussion of the underlying economic system of global capitalism, which I would argue is the root cause of this malaise. The democratic crisis is usually talked of as a separate event to the almost four decades of rapacious wealth and income accumulation by global elites alongside stagnant real wage

Introduction

growth amongst workers and the decline of regular jobs capable of providing a decent income to afford basic necessities for many people on the planet. The threat to regular low-skilled and even more skilled, but routine, work by automation in the future threatens to deepen this jobs crisis, adding more grist to the mill of right-wing populists. The collapse of well-paid and unionized industrial jobs in Europe and North America, and the shift of work to China and other parts of the Global South, has fuelled a reaction against globalization, or at least its neoliberal free trade form, which right-wing autocrats, rather than a more progressive left, have capitalized on. A slide into a dark Fascistic politics reminiscent of the 1930s is not far away unless we are able to fashion a very different kind of economy to the one we have now.

Not only is there little sense of the economic fundamentals, but there is seldom much introspection among the liberal establishment on their own role in fashioning the current democratic crisis. While acknowledging that political elites have neglected the 'white working class', a rather simplistic and racist trope in itself, there is little critical reflection on the existing economic order that underpins this sense of disconnect. When genuinely radical popular policies such as more progressive tax regimes, dramatically raising minimum wages, a Green New Deal, or creating democratic public ownership are mooted, they continue to be derided or ignored by the liberal political establishment and its shrinking support base.[1] There is still a commitment not to interfere with 'business as usual'.

The roots of this liberal democratic crisis go back to the 1990s and the centre left's embrace of economic policies that largely served global business interests. While Margaret Thatcher famously announced in 1981 that 'there is no alternative' to business-friendly, market-driven economic policies, it is the acceptance of her creed by the governments of Blair, Clinton, Schroeder, Jospin and other supposed progressives that have arguably contributed as much to our current impasse. The centre left's headlong embrace of economic deregulation, privatization and marketization, now collectively described as neoliberalism, and the retreat from a traditional concern with social justice and income redistribution, leave many lower income groups bereft of political power and support. The argument made then was that, in the face of globalization, old left policies no longer worked because business would go elsewhere if threatened; though like many compelling 'common sense' narratives, there is little 'real-world' evidence to back this up.[2] Instead, the

Introduction

centre left told us, progressives should provide a favourable environment to attract business which would lead to more tax revenues that could then be spent on public services. The financial crisis was the end game of this laissez-faire equivocation, though many still seem dangerously unaware of this.

The retreat from democratic scrutiny in economic policy

The espousal of neoliberal policy doctrine went hand in glove with the evacuation of democratic decision making from critical spheres of public life – especially economic policy – and their delegation to experts and technocrats. The best example is the tendency for politicians to make central banks 'independent'. This is generally seen by mainstream media in a positive light. Surely it is just 'good governance' to put the setting of interest rates – critical for the wider economy in establishing the terms on which individuals and businesses are able to borrow and invest money – in the hands of 'independent' experts rather than interfering politicians? Those experts will take the longer view compared to the short-termist electioneering of career politicians.

Introduction

Like many superficially compelling tropes, it falls apart under more critical scrutiny. For sure, it is frequently the case that politicians operate on short-term electoral cycles and many are driven by their own political advantage, rather than the greater good of securing sustainable and equitable economic development. Instead, why not let independent experts who have the requisite skills and knowledge take the key decisions for the longer term. But this begs the question: who do these 'independent experts' themselves represent? Are they themselves neutral arbiters of the common good? And, how might they make decisions on behalf of a public that is so diverse and multifaceted? While many individual politicians are of course driven by short-term and often quite narrow electoral interests, they are at least in their position because of some form of democratic process.

The argument for independence would have more force if the subsequent expert institutions drew upon a diversity of knowledge, experience and skills, accepting that the economy has many constituent parts, different needs and ways of life. Yet, policy makers are typically drawn from a narrow elite technocratic class rather than being reflective of society as a whole. The current membership of the Bank of England's Monetary Policy Committee (staffed by eight men and one woman, all of whom are white) can broadly be described as financial elites, four of whom come from the private banking sector (investment rather than retail), one from a career within the Bank of England, two from the UK Treasury and two academic economists, one of whom had previously worked at the Federal Reserve Bank in Boston.

This is an extraordinarily narrow collective world view and in no way reflects the diversity of the United Kingdom, with no representative who can claim to speak for the UK's minority nations and regions outside of London and the South East. Central bank independence is but one important element of a much broader trend for economic decision making – there is a revolving door between senior economic ministry positions and the financial sector in many countries – to become increasingly concentrated within a narrow elite removed from public scrutiny and democratic control. In the UK, this has meant that the growing dominance of financial activities over the broader economy (Lapavitsas 2013) is exacerbated by the values of the financial class shaping policy in its own image and to its own advantage.

Introduction

Making the case for economic democracy in the twenty-first century

Confronting the various crises and challenges that we face requires tackling both the accumulation of wealth and the control of economic decision-making processes by financial and business interests. This is the renewed project for economic democracy that I outline in this book.

Conventionally, economic democracy is often conflated with industrial democracy or workplace democracy; the extent to which workers have ownership and democratic control over their labour, rather than subservience to managers and private owners. Its subject matter has typically been concerned with collective bargaining rights and employee participation in the workplace, or with the promotion of cooperatives and employee ownership. Matters are further complicated by the existence of the term 'social democracy', a dominant reformist trend in labour and progressive left politics in the period after 1945 (though having a much longer lineage) and which also has its roots in workplace trade union struggles and labour politics. While the workplace and the sphere of industrial democracy remain a critical concern here, I want to take a broader and more holistic view (see also Malleson 2013), exploring how we create a democratic economy as a more socially and ecologically sustainable alternative to the status quo. This requires consideration of how economic processes in their entirety, and not just in the workplace, are subject to collective decision making and ownership, widespread public deliberation and full democratic participation (Pateman 1970).

I also emphasize the importance, in a fully functioning economic democracy (Dahl 1985), of recognizing the rights of individuals in all their diversity to participate in this collective process. The individual is largely missing from earlier conceptions of economic democracy, particularly workplace-based forms, which have tended to see it as a collective project on behalf of workers as a class. This has been an error and a gift to the those on the right who have been able to equate the individual, freedom and capitalism – around notions of private property rights – at the expense of the common good. Here I wish to go beyond the needless antagonism between individual and collective rights. If we accept that, as individuals, all our economic activities involve social interaction and cooperation, then it follows that to realize our individual economic rights in a positive fashion – that does not at the same time infringe on the rights of others – inevitably requires forms of collective organization and public engagement.

In developing my argument here, there are three key 'pillars' that run through the remainder of the book. The first is the centrality of individual economic rights. Democracy, as the political theorist Robert Dahl reminds us (Dahl 1985), is fundamentally about individuals being able to exercise their democratic rights by participating in decision-making processes. This applies equally to the economy as it does to other areas of polity and society. Second, and following on from the discussion above, securing these rights requires much greater collective and democratic ownership of firms, resources and property than exists at present. I go on to argue that this requires a mixed (markets and planning) economy of diverse collective ownership as an alternative organizational ethos to the private property dominance of global capitalism. Alongside and enabling these first two pillars is a third: the need to widen and deepen public engagement and participation in decision making to cultivate a more democratic and deliberative political economy. Taken together, these are fundamental supports for transcending capitalism and moving towards a democratic economy.

Following this Introduction, the book consists of

four chapters. In the next chapter, I explore a brief history of economic democracy, movements for workplace and industrial democracy, their achievements and weaknesses, as well as the successes but also democratic failings of social democracy. I then develop my own framework for economic democracy, founded around the three pillars in chapter 2. Chapter 3 explores examples of existing initiatives and practice for each of the three pillars, while in the Conclusion, I restate my argument and explore some of the policies required to enact my broader sense of economic democracy. I also consider some of the constraints and vested interests to be overcome and how we might mobilize to make the democratic economy a reality.

1

A Brief History of Economic Democracy as Industrial Democracy

Introduction

It is important to remember that demands for more democratic economies and egalitarian societies always involve struggles from below against dominant elites. Even the more enlightened elite projects, such as liberal Keynesianism, are, from a democratic point of view, incomplete and, from the point of view of economic democracy, unsatisfactory solutions aimed at preserving elite power and control over 'the masses' rather than transforming the economy in a more democratic and egalitarian fashion.[1] Marx and Engels' basic dictum is that: 'the whole history of mankind ... has been a history of class struggles, contests between exploiting and exploited, ruling and oppressed classes' (Marx and Engels 1848: 8). Those at the sharp end of oppression and exploitation by the ruling class must always struggle and organize collectively to secure basic economic and social rights that improve their conditions of existence.

The history of capitalism is replete with such struggles. Even prior to the industrial revolution, movements such as the Diggers during the English Civil War argued for a radical redistribution of wealth and ownership in opposition to elite attempts to appropriate land. Struggles for economic democracy up until the 1970s tended to be of two kinds: movements to assert rights to common or cooperative ownership; and attempts by workers, usually collectively through trade unions, to regain more autonomy or self-government of their own labour against management encroachment.[2]

In this chapter I briefly review these past struggles for social justice from the perspective of economic democracy.[3] While recognizing the importance of their achievements, my argument is that they were restricted and partial forms of economic democracy. The emergence in the post-1945 period of a strong labour movement across many economies in the Global North made huge advances in reducing inequalities and developing modern welfare states. It also achieved greater rights and participation in the workplace, though still short of the forms of economic democracy advocated here. But it centred around an exclusionary, predominantly white, male form of trade unionism with its roots in the (predominantly industrial) workplace at the expense of other groups, especially women, migrants, ethnic minorities and domestic labour. By the 1970s, many of the gains made by labour and the working class were under attack, and subsequent advances made by neoliberals were in part enabled by the lack of a commitment to a more deep-seated economic democracy both within the workplace and in the wider economy.

Struggles for economic democracy in the nineteenth century

Struggles for economic democracy in the nineteenth century were framed against the backdrop of industrialization and urbanization, beginning in Europe before spreading outwards to the rest of the world. These represented attempts by workers and communities to exert local collective agency to improve what were often appalling material conditions of poverty and exploitation. But they also articulated more radical visions for new forms of society, challenging the rapacious and destructive forms of capitalism then emerging. Of the two traditions of economic democracy that emerged, one sought to create cooperative forms of ownership within the developing factory system, espousing alternative values around mutualism and solidarity; and the second, rooted in growing trade union action and strength, sought to challenge and even overthrow the capitalist control of the economy itself. While they often operated together through the same actors and places, they could also be antagonistic to one other, particularly evident in 'successful' revolutionary states such as the Soviet Union and China, where state ownership 'on behalf of the workers' ended up brutally extinguishing older forms of mutualism.

Cooperativism originated in the textile districts of northern England and central Scotland in the early 1800s, associated with emblematic figures such as Robert Owen and the Rochdale Pioneers, but also had roots in France where a separate tradition of skilled workers' cooperatives emerged (Zamagni and Zamagni 2011). Elsewhere, cooperative banks and credit unions developed in Germany and northern Italy, with cooperative movements also becoming established in North America by the early 1900s. The central economic concern for cooperatives was to develop autonomous organizations to

meet basic collective needs, independent of dominant local employers, notably in the provision of
cheap food but over time expanding to include
housing, finance and even medical care. Politically,
cooperatives aimed at producing more harmonious
reciprocal societies of mutual care in opposition
to the individualistic and exploitative nature of
capitalism.

Mass industrial trade unionism, supplanting a
craft-based and conservative labour aristocracy
(Hobsbawm 1964), grew in strength as a collective
democratic challenge to privately owned capitalism from the 1870s onwards, once again emerging
in the UK but quickly spreading across Western
Europe and North America. With the growth of
large-scale factory organization and massive concentrated workforces in heavy engineering, coal
and steel, shipbuilding and armaments, linked to
a creeping militarism and imperialism, collective
action around workplace-based trade unionism
became the critical sphere for social and political mobilization. While the cooperative movement
persisted and remained strong, particularly in rural
areas, it became subsumed as a focus for social and
economic reform by a workplace-based urban class
politics.[4]

In the context of my argument here, both of

these traditions were primarily 'collectivist' projects for social justice, focused on improving the conditions of communities and workers at the sharp end of an unregulated capitalized society. To varying degrees, they also represented movements for economic democracy in challenging capitalist control both in the workplace and wider economy. But, as collectivist projects, they neglected individual rights and their underpinning values of liberty and freedom were downplayed as elements of the broader struggle. The third enlightenment aspiration for equality, but conceived of largely in class or collective terms, became dominant.

The growth of a social democratic labour politics in the twentieth century

The continued growth of an industrial proletariat, mass trade unions and the successful growth of Labour and Social Democratic parties in the first decades of the twentieth century created further momentum around this second form of collectivism. The increased agglomeration of industry in key urban centres, with new consumer industries (notably automobiles) creating further massive concentrations of workers alongside the older industrial sectors, made it easy to organize collective action against a common enemy to improve wages and conditions. As capitalist organizations grew, merged and developed into more centralized national corporate oligopolies, trade unions themselves developed national and regional centres for co-ordinating workplace-based struggles and campaigns.

Growing trade union strength, mass disruption to industry and even the overthrow of capitalism itself, with revolutions in Russia and the threat of them elsewhere, particularly in Germany and Italy, were all factors that encouraged many business elites to side with Fascism against democracy in the 1920s and 1930s. This, together with the effects of the Great Depression, left capitalism in disrepute at the end of the Second World War and working-class organizations newly empowered. Outside the Communist Bloc, historic class compromises between workers, unions and employers were struck that redistributed income between rich and poor through progressive taxation policies (see figure 1), provided employees with enhanced rights at work and increased social welfare provision alongside a Keynesian influenced commitment to full employment policies.

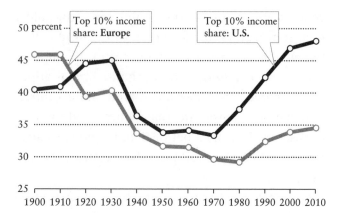

Figure 1. Income Inequality in Europe and the United States, 1900–2010: Share of Top Income Decile in Total Pre-Tax Income

Source: Piketty and Saez (2014: 838).

These represented considerable and historically unprecedented gains for organized labour and the working class as a whole. Not only did working and living conditions improve dramatically but trade unions became recognized in many countries by governments as legitimate social actors. There were two developments in particular that symbolized the changes to capitalist political economy in the post-1945 era: widespread nationalization programmes that transferred whole sectors of the economy into public ownership; and the introduction of co-determination principles in many

European countries that gave workers and trade unions unprecedented rights over how their labour was managed and organized.

Outside the Communist Bloc, where entire economies were taken over by the state, though far removed from any semblance of economic democracy, nationalization programmes were also enacted throughout the capitalist world, in countries as diverse as Argentina, France, India, South Korea and the UK. In the UK, nationalization was brandished as a 'socialization' policy of the new Labour Government in 1945, delivering on the Party's promise to deliver 'common ownership of the means of production'. While it did transfer two million workers into public ownership, helped improve pay and working conditions and provide cheaper and universal services for working-class groups – significant achievements in themselves – it did little to deliver worker empowerment or participation in economic decision making. State enterprises continued to be run by a managerial class – many from the private companies of the previous era – in a top-down fashion with little decision-making power for workers.[5]

Trade union organizations were certainly strengthened and collective bargaining increased across the broader economy, but trade union leadership and the Labour Party hierarchy set their face against giving workers or citizens any real voice in the new public enterprises, let alone the kinds of decentralized, grassroots industrial democracy advocated by those such as G.D.H. Cole (1920). In a telling aside, the future Labour leader Hugh Gaitskell wrote scathingly in 1949 to the minister responsible for nationalization, Herbert Morrison: 'to the effect that TU representatives should be placed on the Boards with the right of members to recall such TU representatives as and when considered necessary is a more extreme example of syndicalist tendencies than anything yet put forward' (Saville 1993: 59). Where trade unionists were appointed to boards, they tended to be right-wing establishment figures such as Sir Joseph Hallsworth (NCB) and Lord Citrine (British Electricity Authority) (Fishman 1993).

In France, where a similar widespread nationalization programme took place, there was more commitment to elected representatives on company boards, alongside separate legislation establishing *comités des entreprise* in 1945, which introduced works councils for all firms with over 50 employees (Cumbers 2019). Over time, however, an elite class of state bureaucrats came to dominate company decision making, and whilst a semblance of industrial democracy remains, most French state-owned companies today operate little differently from privately owned corporations.

The shift towards co-determination across Europe after the Second World War was probably more decisive in the development of economic democracy than nationalization experiences. Where nationalization was accompanied by strong co-determination principles, for example in Austria and Norway, key sectors saw significant advances in employee participation in the workplace. Even in West Germany, where the early centre right governments successfully blocked state intervention and ownership in favour of a social market model, grassroots trade union action in the late 1940s secured legislation to introduce worker representation on company boards in the coal and steel sectors, extending to the rest of the economy by the 1970s. This transformed the industrial relations environment from one of 'authoritarian management and fierce resistance' to the 'nucleus of social partnership in the German economy' (Weitbrecht and Müller-Jentsch 2003: 42).

Such developments were unprecedented in providing workers with a decision-making voice over the use of their labour.[6] But the achievements of Western European co-determination should not be overstated. Many on the left have been rightly critical of its ability to deliver real decision-making power to workers, given the common experience for worker directors to be co-opted into managerial processes rather than providing an independent worker voice. Moreover, the leadership of social democratic and labour parties tended to prioritize the other important social goals of full employment and income redistribution rather than extending and deepening workplace democracy.

The Meidner Plan and the high tide of twentieth-century social democracy

Sweden is rightly acknowledged for its more progressive approach to economic and social rights. What is often forgotten is that this reputation was founded on the back of a very militant labour movement, against hostile anti-union employers, which made significant gains in the 1920s and 1930s, rather than some innate Scandinavian cultural tendency towards social compromise. The Saltsjöbaden Agreement in 1938 gave workers economic rights as social partners at the national level, as well as representation on company boards, although leaving ownership of the main enterprises in the hands of private capital

(Pontusson 1984). It was also in Sweden that one of the most radical practical programmes to give workers greater collective ownership of the economy was launched in the 1970s: the Meidner Plan, named after its main author, economist and trade union researcher Rudolf Meidner.[7]

Described as 'The most explicit attempt to transfer the control of capital to labour' (Minns 1996: 44), the Plan proposed to force companies to dedicate 20 per cent of profits each year to wage-earner funds. It was originally intended to help maintain Sweden's Solidarity Wage system, which reduced wage inequalities in the 1960s, but was coming under pressure with the economic downturn in the 1970s. The primary objective had been redistributive; correcting for the potential for corporations to hoard profits at a time when the government, fearful of inflation in a full employment economy, was seeking to impose wage restraint. Despite its modest origins, Meidner had calculated that, if implemented in its entirety, all large corporations would be worker owned in thirty-five years. The shares would be held collectively by unions on behalf of workers and administered at the regional level. Unfortunately, after sustained employer lobbying, the Social Democratic government introduced a pale shadow of the Plan, a tax on excess profits, producing a much smaller fund which was privatized following the election of a right-wing government in 1992 (Gowan and Viktorsson 2017).

In retrospect, the Meidner Plan represented the high tide for twentieth-century economic democracy in its industrial and social democratic form; notably it was to be controlled by the unions rather than by the workers themselves. As such, it lacked a deeper commitment to grassroots economic democracy.[8] But the Plan was also reflective of pressures for change from below, coinciding with the emergence of a strong 'rank-and-file' movement across Western Europe challenging both union leaderships and corporate capitalism, arguing for more radical forms of workplace democracy. In the UK, for example, the Institute for Workers Control and the Alternative Economic Strategy group of the Labour Party argued for much greater democratic control and strategic planning of both the nationalized industries and the broader economy. The 1974–9 Labour Government initially committed itself to extending public ownership and developing economic democracy legislation. It went as far as launching a Committee of Inquiry on Industrial Democracy, the Bullock Report, which, although never enacted, advocated among other things worker-directors and new company legislation to recognize employee as well as shareholder interests in corporate governance.

The convenient fiction of Thatcher's property-owning democracy

As is now well documented, the post-1945 social contract between unions and employers came under increasing strain in the late 1960s with global competition from newly emerging industrializing countries and increasing employer unwillingness to cede ground to workers on pay and conditions. The subsequent flight of multinational capital to cheaper labour in the Global South, deindustrialization and massive job losses in the trade union heartlands of North America and Western Europe, served to undermine the gains made by workers and trade unions. In this context, a right-wing political project around a 'neoliberal' free market economy, championed in government by Margaret Thatcher and Ronald Reagan, also began to gain ground. The political ascendancy of this project in the 1980s decisively shifted the balance of power in the workplace and broader economy back towards employers and corporations.

A Brief History of Economic Democracy

Although there was little real interest among neo-liberals in economic democracy, fixated as they were on attacking trade unions and the post-war welfare state, for electoral reasons Thatcher in particular felt compelled to offer her own narrative of the 'property-owning democracy'. The 1980s privatizations of the UK's nationalized industries, later imitated globally, were successfully marketed (from an electoral point of view helping Thatcher win three general elections) as exercises in popular capitalism and the construction of a private shareholder democracy. The fact that the majority of individual shareholdings were sold on almost immediately as share prices rocketed (partly because they were deliberately priced too low),[9] and the longer term trend in share ownership in the British economy has been the takeover by foreign private and state corporations, is an inconvenient detail that has been glossed over (figure 2).

Such changes were cloaked in the Hayekian[10] language of freedom, individualism and rational choice for which markets and private property rights were seen as crucial. In the context of the Cold War and the absence of democracy in Soviet-style communism, there was an intuitive appeal for many in these arguments. Simultaneously, anti-trade union rhetoric that cast them as the opponents of

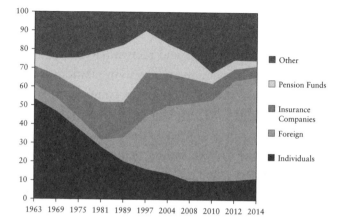

Figure 2. Ownership of Share Capital in UK's Quoted Companies 1963–2014

Source: Office for National Statistics 2016.

democracy and freedom, as in the freedom not to go on strike, directed by Thatcher at the miners during the national strike in 1984–5, were marshalled against a backdrop of industrial militancy and sense of national crisis.

But the kinds of freedoms being evoked here are profoundly negative, linked to a demonization of the other, a political retreat from a sense of the common good and cloaked in a narrow and highly 'economized' sense of the individual (Brown 2015). The selfish individual in the competitive market-place, when mixed in with growing inequalities and

31

a nativist politics in response to globalization, helps exacerbate divisions within society, reproducing patriarchy, xenophobia and racism. Declining jobs, insecure employment and falling living standards can be blamed on 'others' who are in competition with the male 'white working class' for increasingly scarce employment opportunities rather than challenging the underlying fundamentals of global capitalism, where that very same group are also exploited. Four decades on, the outcome of neoliberalism is to take the liberal creed far away from the classical enlightenment liberalism of Locke and Rousseau, or even Adam Smith and John Stuart Mill. Democracy itself becomes hollowed out with this perverted sense of the individual. Meanwhile, the actual experience has been a massive shift in economic power to corporations, institutional shareholders and financial interests, leaving most individuals powerless. Any sense of freedom or liberty for the majority has dissipated under the coercion of free market rule.

'Stale, male and pale': the exclusions of twentieth-century industrial democracy

While the neoliberal espousal of markets, individualism and freedom as the route to democracy looks increasingly empty and spent as a political creed, amidst the deepening social divisions of the twenty-first century, we should acknowledge that the ability of the right to appropriate these terms effectively for four decades was in large part due to the left's failure to develop more genuine forms of economic democracy beyond a narrow workplace politics allied to a managerialist social democracy. Neoliberals could then successfully portray this as self-serving of vested interests (i.e. state bureaucrats, unions and their predominantly male blue-collar members) while also anti-individual and anti-freedom.

The calamitous effects of economic globalization and deindustrialization on the core industrial working-class constituency in the 1980s demonstrated the weakness of this position. Unions have been forced to come to terms with a shrinking base, with, as a consequence, declining influence and power both in the workplace and the wider economy. In this respect, there have been repeated calls for union renewal, the re-democratization of the union movement itself and the building of a broader social movement unionism that reaches out to tackle gender and racial divides while moving into new expanding sectors of the economy, notably personal care and services but also distribution and logistics (Moody 2018).

From a democratic perspective, the prioritization of economic rights and social empowerment through the workplace and trade union representation was primarily to the benefit of a male, industrial and predominantly white working class at the expense of other social groups, notably women, non-whites and a contingent labour force of migrant workers. After the Second World War, as economies were rebuilt and growth returned, in Western Europe and North America a growing immigrant workforce was used to deal with labour supply shortages; a 'reserve army' with low wages and poor working conditions, bereft of the political and economic rights of the established unionized workforce (Castles 2006). Although there were important exceptions and continuing traditions of international labour solidarity,[11] trade unions and their members were often complicit in the marginalization of immigrant and non-white groups from more skilled and better paid jobs (Featherstone 2019). The post-1945 model was also highly gendered, predicated predominantly on the political subject of the male breadwinner at the expense of equal recognition of women in the labour market or workplace (Lewis 1992).[12]

There were important responses to and new struggles over this situation both within and outside the labour movement with the emergence of grassroots campaigns by women and non-white ethnic groups for equal rights and representation at work. These secured important gains in the 1970s and 1980s, although pay gaps and inequality continue to persist into the present. Another critical development was a broader movement for women's rights, initiated in the United States that contested patriarchal norms and women's role in the family and control over reproductive issues, but gradually extending to a movement for economic and social equality. An important aspect of this movement was asserting the centrality of the care and reproductive work of households (done overwhelmingly by women and largely unpaid and poorly paid) as the bedrock for the rest of economy (see James 2008). The continuing prioritization of economic rights and social empowerment through the workplace – as a white male preserve in most advanced capitalist countries into the 1980s – ultimately reflected a constrained and exclusionary agenda for economic democracy.

Conclusion

The impressive strides made towards greater equality and social welfare in the middle years of the twentieth century across much of the industrialized world were only possible through a grassroots mobilization among the industrial working class around important collective rights and principles to challenge the power of elites. As we have seen, this was always a rather restricted form of economic democracy built around the industrial, male and predominantly white working class. The focus on collective worker rights had both a progressive and a darker side. On the one hand, it showed the 'associational power' (Wright 2001) of organized labour in the way that united, mass collective action can mobilize and challenge economic elites. But without a commitment to the broader universal and internationalist principles of individual economic and social rights, this collectivism can turn into the protection of particular groups and interests at the expense of others.

Addressing some of these weaknesses and exclusions, a renewed case for economic democracy must develop new thinking around how to bring collective struggles together with an agenda around universal individual rights which also respects the diverse social interests and identities that contribute to economic life. The confidence trick played by neoliberalism was to separate the individual from society. This was most famously expressed in Margaret Thatcher's aphorism that 'there is no such thing as society', legitimizing the erosion of a political commitment to the common good. A radical economic democracy needs to bring these elements back together; a task that we begin in the next chapter.

2

The Three Pillars of Economic Democracy

In this chapter, I set out the basic framework for rethinking economic democracy. Going beyond the earlier forms of industrial or workplace-based economic democracy discussed in the last chapter, this consists of the three fundamental pillars identified in the Introduction – individual economic rights, collective and democratic ownership and more deliberative and participatory economic practices – which I argue are central to the task of creating a more democratic economy (table 1).

Through the first pillar, I emphasize the rights of individuals to both exercise control over their labour and participate more broadly in economic decision making. I should stress from the outset that my perspective on individual economic rights is diametrically opposed to the atomized individual of mainstream economics and the neoliberal

The Three Pillars of Economic Democracy

Table 1. Three Pillars of Economic Democracy

Individual economic rights	Rights of labour versus property rights
	Self-government of labour in and beyond the workplace
	Resources and skills for flourishing + 'choiceworthy' lives
Diverse forms of collective ownership	Collective 'appropriation rights' over the social surplus
	Construction of the common good versus elite vested interests
	Reinvigorate democratic state planning
Creating deliberative and knowledgeable publics	Rights for collective action
	Active and contested civil society
	Principles of pluralism, diverse and competing perspectives

imagination. By recognizing instead, the socialized individual, who is part of a broader public concerned with the sustainable and fair reproduction of society, the first pillar runs alongside the second and third pillars which are concerned with how we construct democratic, collective and deliberative economic institutions.

Regarding the second key pillar, my concern is with how different forms of collective ownership can be developed to both deepen democracy in the workplace but also allow the fullest participation of all social groups in economic decision making. In this regard, and in contrast to some monolithic state socialist projects of the past, I underline the importance of both public and cooperative forms of ownership to enhancing economic pluralism and democracy.

For the third pillar, I sketch out some of the dangers of the regime of post-democratic economic governance that have emerged with neoliberalism and, more recently, austerity policies. In opposition, I advocate a very different radical democratic and participatory vision of the economy founded on a critical and knowledgeable public sphere that requires deliberative governance institutions that are capable of generating diverse and competing perspectives.

Individual economic rights and self-government

What is the place of the individual within debates about economic democracy? This is a question all too frequently neglected by socialists, social democrats and all those on the left concerned with creating a more egalitarian, just and sustainable economy. Many of us – myself included – working within the broad tradition of radical political economy pioneered by Marx, have tended to perceive injustice primarily as a problem of class

40

conflict in a collective sense. This neglect has ceded important ground around the individual, but also the related themes of liberty and democracy, to the right. Neoliberals have successfully colonized this space in the past four decades, strengthening their hegemony in the aftermath of the collapse of Soviet Communism as an anti-democratic oppositional pole of 'actually existing socialism'.

My starting point takes the basic premise that democracy is a hollow shell if it does not enhance and protect the rights of individuals, whatever their gender, ethnicity, sexuality or even religious persuasion. Economic democracy, viewed in this light, is as much about securing individual rights, as the collective rights of a class or group. It is also about protecting the rights of minorities, as well as delivering more egalitarian outcomes on behalf of an exploited mass versus an empowered elite. Clearly, there will always be difficult trade-offs and balances to be struck in practice, but this is an important foundation.

Theorists such as Amartya Sen and Martha Nussbaum have emphasized that individual freedoms can only be fulfilled where citizens have the economic resources, competences and capabilities to flourish. Rather than the rational choice of individual consumers, this is a form of economic citizenship that is about providing people with the means, resources and capabilities to lead what Burczak (2006) terms 'choiceworthy lives'. People require the freedom – as far as is possible – to develop their full potential in a way that they see fit. This means, in a properly functioning democratic society, all individuals should have, in the words of the eminent liberal political theorist Robert Dahl, 'access to a minimum supply of resources ... for the exercise of democratic rights, for example – but not the right to acquire an indefinitely large supply of resources' (Dahl 1985: 81–2).

Once we have established this basic premise, another important question emerges: what are the constraints to individuals exercising their economic rights? In this respect, and as alluded to by Dahl, a basic contradiction arises between enabling all individuals to have access to the resources to flourish and allowing some individuals to inexorably accumulate wealth without restriction over time. In other words, inequality and private wealth acquisition are incompatible with a proper democracy. This situation is, of course, what currently exists under a turbo-charged deregulated global capitalism, which defends the sanctity of private property in the face of gross inequalities in wealth and resources. The number of billionaires has doubled since the financial crisis at a time when austerity policies are eviscerating welfare budgets, and the twenty-six richest people own as much as half the world's population (Elliott 2019). The world's poorest half receive 12 cents out of every dollar in global growth compared to 27 cents captured by the top 1 per cent (Alvaredo et al. 2017). While the rich are encouraged to accumulate vast private wealth, a significant proportion of the world's population are unable to access the resources and income to live flourishing lives that would equate with a fully functioning democratic citizenship. As Andrew Sayer's excellent recent book suggests, if we are committed to economic democracy and social justice, in a fundamental sense we really can't afford the rich (Sayer 2014).

The necessity of labour self-government

Capitalism – as an economic system – in its very structures and underlying processes produces inequalities; in a world of finite resources the acquisition of private property by a few over time erodes the ability of others to have the resources to live, let alone flourish. Social democracy and Keynesian liberalism, with their redistributive tax measures and forms of progressive government intervention, can modify and alleviate the worst excesses but they do not get to the heart of the problem. Only a more transformative economic democracy can do this. But, how do we do this in a way that also respects individual economic rights and freedoms rather than a purely class-based attack on wealth and privilege that history suggests can produce new exclusions and injustices?

A crucial insight in this regard is provided by the political economist and philosopher David Ellerman with his deployment of the theory of labour property rights (see Ellerman 1990, 1992). Writing in the early 1990s, in the context of the collapse of Soviet-style socialism and the triumph of Western capitalism, Ellerman highlights the philosophical and political deficiencies of both mainstream economics' defence of capitalism and the alternative critical Marxist perspective. Despite their mutual antipathies, both, according to Ellerman, are guilty of fixating on ownership as the core dynamics of capitalism, rather than the actual employment relationship itself, which for him is the real source of exploitation.

Mainstream economics treats private property rights in a market economy as being the fundamental corner stone of capitalism. Only when rights to private property are assigned and legally protected can individuals engage in free and voluntary exchange. Labour markets are also viewed like any other market, permitting individuals to come together voluntarily to buy and sell labour.

However, as Ellerman and Marx before him make clear, labour is not like any other factor of production but is made up of human beings, who have certain basic rights under classical liberal jurisprudence. This includes the 'property rights' over their own labour as the sentient being responsible for that labour. But under the employment contract in capitalist societies, once human beings voluntarily sell their labour, they are effectively handing over the ownership and control of their labour to the employer. Within a given context, under existing employment contracts, legally the worker must obey the employer. While mainstream economists might reply that people are free to walk away from a punitive employer, this disregards the fundamental reality that the vast majority of people cannot do this as they need paid employment for their livelihood, and it clearly depends on the availability locally of alternative jobs for the same pay. A key point is that this is not a contract between equals; moreover, the property rights of employers are taking precedence over the worker's individual right to control their labour and its product.

Ellerman draws from legal theory with its understanding of humans as responsible and knowing actors – in contradistinction to non-human things, such as other factors of production – to argue that individual workers have certain 'inalienable' rights to the 'appropriation', i.e. ownership and control of both their labour and its product. However, in capitalism, it is the manager or owner of a capitalist firm that has these appropriation rights – to control work and any product and profits deriving from it – rather than labour. But as Ellerman and others point out, this is effectively a legitimized dictatorship of the workplace. Under liberal democratic capitalism, democracy and human rights effectively stop at the workplace.

While Marxist inspired political economy does recognize the nature of the power imbalance in management–labour relations and the potential for exploitation of labour by capitalism to exist – indeed it is one of Marx's fundamental insights – Ellerman claims that the bulk of Marxist theorists misunderstand the source of this exploitation by not differentiating sufficiently between the property rights of ownership and the actual contractual aspect of employment. The latter, what he terms the 'hiring contract', is the key power relationship under capitalism not the former. A system that underpins private property rights as sacrosanct might lead to inequalities and the concentration of land, resources and power, problems that we come to in due course, but it is not the fundamental relation that differentiates capitalism from other social systems, for example slavery or feudalism.

Thus, the twentieth-century socialist fixation on ownership – taking control of the means of production – and transferring this from private to public hands is only a partial solution from an economic democracy perspective if it does not simultaneously transform relationships within the workplace, abolishing the 'hiring contract' between employer and employee; it fails to tackle a key element of capitalist power relations. The relations of 'actually existing' state socialism in the twentieth century in countries as diverse as China, the Soviet Union or even Yugoslavia demonstrated this all too well. From the workers' perspective, one set of 'masters' was replaced by another: private capitalists by state bureaucrats.

For Ellerman, the solution is the democratic enterprise where the relationship between workers and managers is abolished and replaced by self-government by the workers themselves. His arguments link to a much longer tradition of market socialism where cooperatives and self-managed employee ownership (regarded approvingly by nineteenth-century liberals like John Stuart Mill) are viewed as better expressions of economic democracy than state-owned enterprises because they confer on employees ownership rights to their labour. Workers would both control their own labour but also the product of their labour: the wealth and income arising from it; in other words, what are termed 'appropriation rights'.

Individual economic rights beyond the workplace
Developing these arguments further, I would contend that this economic dictatorship extends beyond the workplace under capitalism (particularly of the neoliberal variety) into the economy more generally. As noted above, beyond a small global elite, very few people have the independent wealth to live without selling their labour. In this sense, the compulsion to work to 'earn a living' further limits the voluntary nature of the employment contract and gives the lie to the idea of an 'equal exchange' in the labour market. The post-1945 welfare state and the policy goal of full employment pursued by many governments in the advanced economies up until the 1970s were important political and social mechanisms – under pressure from strong trade union movements – that rebalanced the labour

market considerably in favour of workers with more jobs and fewer workers, while providing some basic income and subsistence independent of paid work.

Subsequently, under neoliberalism, these relatively limited achievements have been under attack and severely curtailed. Alongside restrictions on the rights of unions and workers to undertake collective action, neoliberal labour market policy has focused on reducing restrictions on employers, alongside removing the protections for workers, whilst at the same time introducing increasingly punitive 'workfare' regimes (Peck 2001; Bonoli 2010). The reduction of welfare benefits, as well as making these benefits increasingly linked to the willingness to accept work of any kind, has been a key project for the Thatcherite right. Such developments raise the question of the economic rights and self-governance of all citizens, not just those active in the labour market.

The focus of Ellerman, Dahl and others remains on achieving economic democracy in the workplace, a laudable and important project but still a partial approach to achieving a more holistic economic democracy. In the first place, it is silent on perhaps the most critical work required in the reproduction of society, the labour of housework, which is riven with social inequality. Much of this is undertaken by women or ethnic minorities and is unpaid or carried out by poorly paid and largely unregulated labour. How do we try to address the appropriation rights for this kind of labour? I suggest a solution to this in the next chapter.

A second problem is that it neglects some of the changes that have taken place in the organization of work and employment over the past half century, which require a set of responses beyond the workplace. As we have seen, globalization and deindustrialization combined have reshaped the world of work; a decline in employment in manufacturing and a shift towards services across the advanced economies of the Global North has been accompanied by – and partly caused by – growing competition from and the relocation of work to the Global South. Globally, competition for paid work is increasing; one estimate suggests that the global labour supply – those of working age eligible for work in the capitalist economy – has trebled since 1980 (Standing 2011). At the same time, the availability of permanent paid employment (that pays a decent living wage and gives individuals some kind of security) is declining. Half of all jobs created in the advanced industrial economies since 1980 have been part time, temporary or self-employed (OECD

2015) while more broadly around one quarter of the world's workforce are in permanent contracts (ILO 2015).

Four other processes are worthy of note here. First, since the 1970s, as a response to increasing competition from newly industrializing countries, firms have dramatically changed their labour strategies, making much greater use of flexible workers – those without permanent employment status. A growing global 'precariat' of individuals, perhaps as many as a quarter of the world's workforce, lack secure employment status, are subject to poor wages and working conditions and are devoid of basic employment rights (Standing 2011).

Second, governments have helped facilitate this precarity through new labour laws that have both deregulated the labour market, making it easier for firms to hire and fire alongside reducing welfare and social benefits to those made unemployed. In the UK, an extreme and notorious form has been the 'zero-hours' contract, whereby employers are allowed to hire workers without any guarantee of regular hours per week; the average wage for those on zero-hours contracts is £188 per week compared to £470 for permanent workers (MacKinnon and Cumbers 2019: 184). Many governments (notably the US and UK) have attacked the ability of workers and their unions to organize through draconian legislation favouring employers.

Third, increased automation and technical change in manufacturing and services has further reduced the number of decent jobs available. Although some of the more dystopian predictions of 'the end of work' need to be taken with a healthy pinch of salt, the trends are nevertheless clear, with declining numbers of jobs, particularly for men, and a growing crisis of employment opportunity for younger people (see ILO 2015; Avent 2016).

The final trend has been the collapse in real wage rates (and the massive disparities in income between the global elite and the rest) as a consequence of these changes. A recent report for the US Congress found that real median wages in the US had stagnated between 1979 and 2017, with lower wage workers below the median experiencing a decline in real terms (Donovan and Bradley 2018).

The central take home point here, though, is that in a world of diminishing employment prospects, a project for economic democracy that is fixated solely on self-governance at the workplace risks focusing upon an economy that no longer exists, or would apply only to a core and privileged group while neglecting other kinds of work fundamental to both social reproduction and the basic functioning of the economy. We therefore need to think more holistically about a broader project for individual economic rights for the economy as a whole within and beyond the workplace for all kinds of workers and their dependents. Framed in this way, our focus (returning to Sen and Nussbaum) should be on providing opportunities both for human flourishing but also for the rights of participation and involvement in economic life. In this regard, access to a minimum liveable level of resources becomes critical, not just to provide basic needs for subsistence but also to allow individuals to have the skills, education and competences to make meaningful choices about how they use their labour.

Democratic, collective and diverse public ownership

The insistence on individual economic rights and self-government in a broader sense brings us to our second pillar of economic democracy: the need for democratic and diverse forms of collective ownership. Strong rights to collective action and freedom of association inherent in the ability to form independent trade unions are a critical element that I deal with under the third pillar. Here my focus is with constructing democratic rights for individuals for the ownership and control of labour and the economy in its entirety.

Following Ellerman's logic, this involves a shift away from the corporate or privately-owned firm towards collective forms of ownership that provide self-governance of labour. This may sound counter-intuitive at first, but only if one holds to the mainstream economics perspective of atomized, rational and selfish individuals for whom freedom is about the freedom to own property or engage in selling your labour as an individual rather than in combination. In reality, and one of the fundamental insights of Marx, as individuals our work is always social, dependent upon, and in collaboration with, others. Even the self-employed rely upon other workers to function; taxi drivers need other people to build and maintain the roads that they operate on, even the most digital libertarian tech entrepreneur needs the infrastructure of the internet to be built, maintained and upgraded by other workers. We all require local or city authorities and their employees to provide the infrastructure for us to drink, eat and dispose of our waste, travel to work and much more besides: the basic essentials of life and all the other elements that make life worthwhile (e.g. subsidized sport and recreation, libraries, museums, etc.).

The Three Pillars of Economic Democracy

All work is collaborative, but following Ellerman's arguments, individuals should have the democratic right to have ownership and control of the work that they carry out inside organizations. If one accepts these basic premises, conferring an individual right logically leads to more collective ownership of the economy, where the radical conception of economic liberty can be given proper democratic expression. This right is fundamentally at odds with the rights of the owners and managers of firms to control the labour of others and inevitably requires forms of democratic collective ownership for workers and arguably the eradication of private capitalist employers altogether to fully realize these rights.

From a basic democratic viewpoint, a fundamental flaw in attempts to create collective ownership in many previous forms of social democracy, socialism and communism, as noted above, was the failure to recognize the rights of workers to self-government of their labour and for citizens to participate meaningfully in economic decision making more broadly. The replacement of private ownership with state ownership merely exchanged the property rights of capitalists with those of state elites and bureaucrats. One interesting variant, which continues to inspire many, was the Yugoslav decentralized model of public ownership with self-managed worker

enterprises (Estrin 1991) where workers had considerable autonomy and control, even the ability
to appoint managers. Critically, however, the state
remained the underlying owner of the enterprise,
which tended to encourage short termism with little
incentive for the workforce to think strategically
(Nove 1983; Estrin 1991). Nevertheless, it is worth
pointing out that this self-managed model worked
very well through the 1960s and most of the 1970s,
outperforming many Western European economies
(notably the UK) in terms of economic growth.[1]

Under capitalism, it is private property owners,
those who own capital, land, assets, firms, that
largely appropriate surplus or profit that comes
from productive activity, even though they are
heavily dependent on their workers to produce it.
Progressive taxation by left and centre left governments can redistribute some of this surplus, and
clearly in some Nordic and Western European
countries the state can assume a dominant redistributive form, but more broadly capitalists remain
the ultimate arbiters of how wealth is generated,
how it is used and for what purpose. This is critical
not just in the short term for who receives the lion's
share of income but also in the longer term. Those
that control how the surplus is allocated are the
ones in charge of investment decisions and hence

control all our futures in shaping the trajectory of the economy itself.

For Ellerman, the solution to this dilemma is to give full property and ownership rights of labour – including the appropriation rights – to the 'direct producers'; workers themselves in collective forms of enterprise such as employee-owned firms or producer cooperatives. Some socialists – such as Theodore Burczak (2006) – even contend that a market economy of entirely collectively owned employee enterprises – with an accompanying strong welfare state – would produce a more equitable economy that retained all the positive dynamic, entrepreneurial and self-regulating elements of capitalism.[2] But there are dangers here that such an approach on its own would privilege a new dominant group. While recognizing these ownership rights, it is important also to give democratic voice to other groups and interests beyond the conventional paid workforce.

Another problem is that a focus on the 'direct producers' in visible employment repeats the mistakes of postwar 1945 industrial democracy identified in the previous chapter, effectively devaluing all the other forms of work that contribute to the 'social surplus' or what has been termed our common wealth. Giving appropriation rights just to these workers effectively marginalizes the many other forms of work that contribute to reproduction of society. As George De Martino notes: 'it is not difficult to imagine a society in which the producers of surplus with full and exclusive rights of appropriation live lavish lifestyles at the expense of those who do not (or cannot) participate in its creation' (De Martino 2000: 105–6).

More broadly, and in keeping with the arguments earlier, the right to participate in economic decision making should go beyond regular paid employees. Some of the worst exploitation in the contemporary economy occurs in the sphere of informal, irregular and illegal forms of work. At the same time, privatization and marketization of basic services have hit the poorest in society hardest, particularly through predatory pricing in utility sectors, where corporations abuse their monopoly power with very little agency or redress for the individual consumer. This is particularly the case in services such as water, electricity and heating, where lack of income, and sometimes knowledge and access to the right social networks, means poorer households often default on their payments and are subject to pernicious and more expensive rates, including metering regimes. In contrast, more affluent consumers with higher and stable incomes are able to exercise their consumer choice by setting up cheaper tariff contracts with suppliers. The recognition of such exploitation and its threat to basic human rights has led some countries, including the Netherlands and Uruguay, and indeed some US states, to make water privatization illegal.

Developing a more radical consumer rights agenda is another strong argument for collective democratic ownership. While consumer cooperatives could be encouraged through legislation, the state should also play an important role, particularly in the utility sectors where new forms of democratic public ownership which provide representation for both elected workers and consumer groups could play a critical role in setting longer term strategic agendas to tackle inequality, poverty and climate change.[3]

More generally, the state – and forms of democratic public enterprise – should play a leading role in a collectively owned economy for four important reasons. First, market relations and market values (even under what would undoubtedly be more humane forms of market socialism) should have no role in many areas of life, including essential public utilities (from energy to water to transport) or health, education and social care.[4] There is also a strong case for restrictions on markets, given their destructive evolutionary dynamics and unequal outcomes, in areas such as land, housing and finance. Neoliberalization has extended marketized and profit-driven commercial values into many areas of life where they should have no presence in a civilized society. Other ethics of care, respect and tolerance need institutional and organizational forms that allow them to be harnessed and sustained.

Second, and relatedly, ensuring universal access and provision – and dealing with residual inequalities – can only be achieved by some form of state ownership and cannot be left to decentralized cooperatively run marketized solutions devoid of a broader concern with universal values and the common good. And third, on efficiency grounds, many sectors – for example, the natural monopolies – operate more effectively through planning and co-ordination rather than marketization. This is especially true of many utility sectors which provide a basic unitary service (e.g. water or heat). Despite elaborate attempts to create markets in these sectors, they can in no way be equated with economic activities that provide genuine consumer choice such as buying a pair of shoes (Nove 1983). Finally, democratic forms of public ownership are also a way of ensuring that all citizens – whatever their relationship to the world of work and the formal productive economy – have some opportunity to participate in economic decision making.

I should make clear here that my argument is not that all citizens should have democratic representation and voice in all areas of economic life but that the economy in its entirety should be subject to collective and diverse forms of ownership with much greater levels of participation and scrutiny than exist at present. Tackling the big economic questions facing society today, whether it is strategies to address climate change, the fair allocation of resources according to social needs, or more general macroeconomic questions about the kinds of goods and services that should be produced, requires democratic negotiation and broad public participation, rather than the privilege of private elites furthering their own wealth accumulation.

Over time, this would require replacing our existing predominantly private and corporate economy with what I term here a diverse ecology of democratic collective ownership. This would entail a mixed economy of both planned and market sectors but with a shift towards public, cooperative, employee-owned and community-owned forms of enterprise. While it is important not to be overly prescriptive, given variations in actually existing economies and the inevitable need for pragmatism and experimentation, a sketch of the possible kinds of democratic ownership is offered in table 2.[5] While globalization has greatly restricted the ability of national governments to devise alternative economic models, 'the socialism in one country model', we should remember that the nation state remains the critical scale for economic governance. With the exception of the European Union, and despite the aspiration to global trade regimes, national governments remain the sovereign legal and regulatory bodies to enact systemic change of the kind suggested here. This reality was brought home in the aftermath of the financial crisis when nationalization and state controls re-emerged to counter thirty years of neoliberal myth making about the end of the state. Hence, table 2.2 implies national-level initiatives albeit recognizing broader geographical realities.

The list is indicative rather than exhaustive; for example, there is a need for a much more sustained and deeper debate about democratic ownership and control of the internet, digital commons and the biosphere than is possible here. But it does attempt to give a sense of the possibilities for organizing our economy democratically across a diverse range of sectors to inculcate social and ecological values for

Table 2. A Diverse Ecology of Collective Ownership in a Democratically Regulated Economy

Sector	Type of collective ownership	Institutional and regulatory arrangements
Finance	– national state ownership for monetary policies – national, regional and local state banks for industrial policy/ economic development – cooperatives for housing + community initiatives – employee-owned pension schemes	– strong and effective demarcation of investment + retail banking – outlawing of certain financial 'pirate' practices (e.g. hedge funds, private equity firms) – tight regulation and taxation of financial speculation with international cooperation – regulated markets for retail banking – restrictions on 'usury' and predatory lending
Utility industries (e.g. electricity, water, gas) and transport	– combination of local municipal ownership and national state infrastructure ownership – limited forms of private ownership (e.g. personal motoring)	– strong environmental targets – redistributive policies and subsidies – high taxes for social + environmental 'bads' (e.g. private motoring, fossil fuel use) – legislation to prevent marketization of critical public services – strong social/environmental regulation of private markets in non-monopoly sectors

continued

Table 2. (*continued*)

Sector	Type of collective ownership	Institutional and regulatory arrangements
Public services (e.g. health, education)	– combination of regional/municipal ownership + national state regulatory bodies	– strong national regulatory structure to ensure equal standards between areas – high taxation of private forms and redistribution of income to state-run areas – legislation to prevent marketization
Housing	– local municipal ownership and resident cooperatives	– national level housing federation to promote public and cooperative ownership – tax subsidies for public + cooperative housing projects – legislation for tighter regulation of mortgage financing and private renting
Consumer products (e.g clothing, food and drink, electronic equipment)	consumer + producer cooperatives small and family-owned firms	– ethical trade rules – living wage standards – rights of collective association – tax and other subsidies to stimulate local and carbon-neutral production systems – freely operating markets but subject to strong regulation

| Private services (e.g. hairdressing, car repair, household/building maintenance) | – self-employed, private firms below 20, employee ownership above 20 | Ditto |
| Consumer services (e.g. restaurants, hotels) | – private firms below 20, employee ownership, consumer co-operatives above 20 | |

the common good rather than narrowly commercialized ones to serve elite ends.

Given the monumental failings of the largely private financial sector to deliver economic stability, provide investment for the productive economy or serve the common good, one can imagine a very different set of collectively-owned organizational forms articulating more social and ecological values. State ownership – under democratic control – at different geographical scales could secure broader national macroeconomic objectives (e.g. decent job creation and sustainable development) while also allowing the financing of local democratically negotiated strategies by local and regional public banks. Something very similar already exists in Germany. Cooperative and other forms of mutual funds could meet other needs, such as housing and pensions. Better public oversight, transparency and regulation could also control, and in some cases outlaw, the most nefarious speculative and socially destructive financial practices (e.g. hedge funds that use their market power to destroy productive parts of the economy for short-term financial gain).[6]

The utility and transport sectors are another set of activities that require collective ownership and planning, in what are often natural monopolies, as opposed to privatization and market structures. But there could be a mix of ownership forms that provide greater local democratic control while still having national-level co-ordination and strategic planning. In many other essential public services, marketization and private profit could be outlawed entirely where they infringe on human dignity, care and human flourishing. The US health care system provides the litmus test of how social ills can flow from private and corporate gain, while also being hugely inefficient in comparison with other countries' health systems. The dysfunctional housing market could be transformed into a mixed economy of mutual, public and private forms of ownership with the expansion of social and state ownership providing individuals with real choices about tenure, with mortgages strictly regulated to avoid the worst excesses of predatory lending, usury and speculation in the private sector.

In other sectors, notably consumer goods and personal services, where markets do play a useful function in signalling consumer preferences, we can imagine other forms of collective ownership predominating, such as consumer cooperatives and employee ownership alongside private forms. In many countries, these forms of ownership already flourish, such as the John Lewis Partnership in the

UK or the Mondragon group in Spain. Remaining private enterprises could be subject to much stricter ethical rules relating to environmental and labour standards, fair trade, which could even apply to foreign enterprises supplying to domestic markets, much as EU rules currently do.

One interesting innovation might be to enforce a cooperative rule above a certain size, perhaps twenty employees, whereby enterprises have to convert to some form of democratic employee self-government. This may not be as unpalatable for many businesses as it might seem; many family businesses already do this as a form of succession planning and the UK government introduced a 100 per cent exemption from capital gains tax in 2014 for those setting up employee-owned trusts. In the US, a recent poll commissioned by the Democracy Collaborative found 69 per cent of people in favour of the idea that workers should have first refusal to buy their firms when owners decide to sell or if the firm faces the threat of closure (Gowan 2019). In effect, the benefits of collective democratic ownership are already more accepted than our mainstream media discourse suggests.

The Three Pillars of Economic Democracy

Creating a deliberative and participatory economic democracy

Economic democracy also requires a much deeper level of engagement and participation by the public itself than is currently the case. Hand in hand with the appropriation of wealth by elites is the colonization of debate and the driving out of alternative ways of thinking about the economy. In this regard, the creation of more deliberative and knowledgeable 'publics' is the critical third pillar of economic democracy. To facilitate this, we need a public sphere that enhances and strengthens pluralism and diversity, not just for its own sake but as a way of both realizing democracy and providing a fertile breeding ground for alternative thinking. One of the few socialists to recognize the importance of this in the twentieth century was Otto Neurath who briefly, in the short-lived Bavarian Soviet Republic of the early 1920s, articulated a pluralistic approach to the economy. He was concerned to advance solidarity between different social groups by encouraging a 'multiplicity of ways of life' and 'non-conformism' against authoritarian tendencies (Neurath 1945).

In some ways, the creation of a genuine participatory economic democracy is the most radical proposal of all. Even during the so-called 'golden age' of capitalism in the post-Second World War era (the period of strong European social democracy), economic decision making was dominated by a managerial elite with little consultation or participation of ordinary citizens. The ascendancy of neoliberal governance has greatly accentuated this situation, whereby not only are many spheres of economic policy removed from public participation, but increasingly they are not even considerate legitimate areas for public debate and political contestation. As a recent body of literature now acknowledges, policy formation under neoliberal hegemony has been characterized as a post-democratic or post-political condition (Rancière 2001; Crouch 2004), largely removed from broader public scrutiny by and on behalf of business and financial interests.

As the membership of the monetary policy committee of the Bank of England in the opening chapter demonstrates, there is a lack of diversity of different social groups and alternative economic perspectives. What in the Global South became known as the 'Washington Consensus' – because it was linked to the key global lending institutions of the International Monetary Fund (IMF) and the World Bank (WB) – has emerged almost everywhere as a dominant form of economic governance. Its priority is providing a stable (in aspiration if not in reality) and accommodating environment for multinational business, characterized by pressures to lower taxes, reduce government expenditure in areas outside business support, cuts to welfare that hit the poorest and the privatization of public assets and services that opens up new areas for profit seeking. Running alongside are pressures to deregulate finance and pursue flexible labour market policies.

This amounts to a single 'globalization' model of economic development, predicated upon export-led growth and the attraction of foreign direct investment, rather than the alternative of stimulating local economies on the basis of real social need. Countries or governments that do not conform to these policies risk being disciplined by the IMF and WB, meaning the cutting off of funds for investment, or the flight of money from hyper-mobile financial markets.[7] The evisceration of democracy and local control over economic development has been all too evident for many countries in the Global South since the 1980s, leading to resistance, particularly in Latin America.

The full force of this disciplinary regime was brought home to hitherto relatively privileged European citizens in the wake of the Eurozone crisis when elected governments were forced to adopt punitive austerity measures designed to bail out and appease the very same financial interests that had engaged in reckless lending and speculative activities in the first place. By virtue of their membership of the Euro and the subordination of economic governance to the European Central Bank, to deal with escalating government debt in the wake of the 2007–9 global financial crisis, Greece, Italy, Spain, Portugal and Ireland were forced into government expenditure cuts, privatizations, job shedding and wage reductions of public sector workers by the unelected Troika (ECB, IMF and European Commission) in return for financial aid. Technocratic experts from economics, finance and the elite European civil service applied neoliberal policy nostrums that had already failed miserably elsewhere, helping to both accelerate the recession and causing widespread social misery (Blyth 2013). This has been part of a broader trend away from democratic accountability within the European Union, even leading to the replacement of a democratic government in Italy at one point.

The European Parliament itself, as the main democratic institution, has very little influence on these processes with virtually no independent legislative power. As one commentator rather vividly expresses it, Members of the European Parliament: 'are not the representatives of a sovereign European people, but fart-catchers to the grand functionaries of EU technocracy' (Phillips 2016: 41). With greater European economic integration, national governments have less independent executive power over economic policy. A key initiative was the introduction of the Stability and Growth Pact in 1998, which imposed a debt limit of 3 per cent on all countries, effectively prohibiting more expansionist Keynesian-style economic policy and inscribing a political doctrine and particular policy choice (neo-liberalism) into EU law. Such EU developments are indicative of wider trends. The US Government and that of the UK (despite being outside the Eurozone) have both implemented new legislation since 2010 to enforce austerity policies, which constrict public spending and seriously curtail the conventional policy options (particularly around running government deficits) open to more progressive parties.

While these developments stem from political capture of key institutions and do not take away the need for higher level co-ordination of public policy, in a world where most of our major problems, notably climate change, need global solutions, they do indicate the seriousness of our economic democratic deficit. Addressing it, we clearly need a much greater degree of real democracy to be applied to economic decision making at all levels, from the workplace, to national government spending priorities, to global agreements about the most effective way to limit CO_2 emissions. This requires greater public participation as well a more knowledgeable civil society, capable of contributing to a more deliberative economic decision-making process.

Trade unions and strong collective bargaining rights, so that workers and their representatives can become important social actors in shaping economic processes, are clearly a critical element in all this. But it also requires a much greater commitment by states and their publics to providing resources, institutions and mechanisms for a much more diverse range of actors and organizations to participate in shaping the direction of economic policy.

While there is often a self-serving rhetoric expressed by political and economic elites (and even trade unionists in my experience) that the average worker or citizen does not want to engage more with such technical matters as economic policy, there is little evidence to justify this. Indeed, where people believe participation to be genuine, rather than the faux consultation exercises operating in many existing participation schemes, the evidence points the other way (see Pateman 2012). An example from the UK in the 1970s is the Lucas Plan, a set of diversification proposals put forward by workers when faced with the potential closure of defence company, Lucas Aerospace. As striking as the workforce's ability and ingenuity in identifying more socially useful products was the number, detail and diversity of the proposals. Over 150 in all that included detailed realistic economic and market analysis as well as principles about how work could be re-organized along more cooperative lines and detailed plans for training and skills enhancement of the workforce (Smith 2014).

There is now also a wealth of evidence demonstrating the benefits of greater public participation in the economy. Not only does it increase individual self-esteem, confidence and empowerment, but it also contributes 'on the ground' knowledge to otherwise detached managements (Pateman, 1970; Fung 2004; Menser 2018; Wainwright 2018). There are also good examples of where participatory democratic decision-making practices, involving both workers and users of public services, generate important tacit knowledge that improves an organization's performance. Organized and largely controlled by elites, the contemporary global economy suffers a considerable knowledge deficit in this respect, alongside its democratic deficit. It is not only wealth that is appropriated through our current economic reality but discourses themselves that are controlled and concentrated through elite interests and institutions. Not only has this weakened democracy but it has also led to a narrowing of the range of options and methods used in economic policy, closing down importance sources of knowledge and expertise, some of which reside in the public themselves rather than experts.

One implication of this is that a genuine deliberative public sphere must be alert to the dangers of a false consensus. Public deliberation requires tolerance of competing narratives, where alternative perspectives can be subject to debate, contestation and even conflict between different groups and interests (Mouffe 2005). While in order to progress, economic decision making will ultimately need to be developed in particular directions to address critical social and increasingly ecological issues, this can be done through the negotiation between different positions rather than imposition from above. Although a decision, by its very nature, will ultimately favour some perspectives over others, a more rounded and consultative co-produced process is surely more likely to lead to better outcomes. More broadly, there should be a commitment to keeping decision-making processes open so that new ideas come forward to challenge established wisdom.

Conclusion

In this chapter, I have sought to put forward a new framework for economic democracy around the three pillars of individual economic rights, collective agency and public engagement and deliberation. Meaningful economic democracy essentially has two key components: collective visions of the common good that are given proper space for debate and contestation, and the individual rights to flourish and participate in this space. Neoliberal hegemony and ideology have greatly reduced these elements, with ruthless suppression of alternatives to austerity, a shrinking state and market imperialism. Rather than producing some kind of optimal outcome, it has created growing inequalities and social division, while providing the fertile breeding ground for demagogues.

Against these tendencies, a democratic economy should foster ongoing and dynamic spaces of collective ownership, public debate and ongoing learning. As the philosopher John Dewey famously observed: 'The essential need, in other words, is the improvement of the methods and conditions of debate, discussion and persuasion. That is the problem of the public' (Morris and Shapiro 1993: 187). Dewey's remarks nearly one hundred years ago were aimed at the way that the more progressive aspects of eighteenth-century liberal doctrine had by the early twentieth century given way to a hierarchical set of power structures that served to bolster elites at the expense of the common good. Elites both on the left and right have often treated economic theory and principles as absolute and applied them in doctrinal fashion with devastating effects. Dewey's radical pragmatism reminds us of the importance of a commitment to an ongoing and open process of democratic intellectual enquiry; words as relevant today as they were a century ago.

3

Putting Economic Democracy into Practice

Having established the basic pillars of economic democracy, I now explore how these might be put into practice. Regarding the first pillar, I identify and evaluate some of the important experiments in creating more individual economic security and autonomy, with a particular emphasis on the proposal for a universal basic income (UBI). With regard to the second pillar, I survey some recent initiatives around democratic collective ownership under construction in a diverse range of countries in response to the failings of privatization. I also focus in on the Mondragon Cooperative in the Basque Region in Spain as an example of a successful worker cooperative network that could be emulated elsewhere, as well as the Danish model of local public and cooperative ownership that has done so much to make the country a world leader

79

in renewable energy. Linked to the third pillar, I will explore attempts at creating more deliberative and participatory forms of economic decision making such as participative budgeting in Latin America and citizens councils and referenda. I also consider some new constitutional movements that seek to give citizens more voice and participation over the national political economy, to make higher level processes of economic governance more accountable, transparent and accessible to citizens. Inevitably, given space constraints, the approach will be broad brush and illustrative, leaving out the myriad of other interesting alternative experiments that could be drawn upon (e.g. Wright 2011) to facilitate a shift towards a more democratic economy.

Institutions for implementing individual self-governance and economic freedom

As we saw earlier, the dominant approach to labour market policy pursued in the wealthier global economies, and indeed actively encouraged by the OECD, IMF and EU, has been to decisively transfer the balance of power away from employees towards employers. Strategies to deregulate and make employment more flexible – code for making it easier to hire and fire workers – have gone alongside a more general and punitive attack on welfare benefits and subsidies for those not in paid work. We are clearly moving a long way from the Ellerman ideal of democratic labour self-governance.

Reversing this trend requires radical thinking and action. One proposal gaining prominence is a universal basic income (UBI). Although it has different variants and names, at heart the UBI provides a guaranteed income for all individuals in society, irrespective of income, wealth or employment situation and, as such, has an intuitive appeal here. Under some proposals, a UBI could also be allocated to children but held in trust until they reach a responsible age. While there are debates about the level that it should be set at, the more progressive supporters tend to agree that it should be sufficient to meet basic needs like shelter, food and clothing.

While recognizing some of the problems involved, of which more below, I would endorse the UBI here for its potential to create real economic freedoms and social empowerment. In his excellent summary, Erik Olin Wright (2011) suggests six positive reasons to support it. The first resonates strongly with the arguments for individual economic freedom made here: that UBI strikes at the heart of the power that capitalism and private employers hold over individual workers, the compulsion to sell your labour to survive. A UBI breaks this link and puts people in control of their labour.

Second, a UBI could also reduce inequalities between jobs in the labour market, raising the wages of the more menial and unpleasant work tasks (because people are less compelled to accept any job to make ends meet). It might prompt technological innovation to eliminate many such jobs, providing a 'humanizing bias' to economic decision making rather than the labour-saving cost minimization rationality of business. Third, it holds out the promise of eliminating poverty without the privations of means testing, as long as progressive taxes remain on earned income. That would mean no 'poverty traps' either; no disincentive to earn additional income by losing welfare payments. Fourth, it would be a means of recognizing the unpaid work around domestic labour and social reproduction, providing economic security for capitalism's 'hidden workforce'.

Fifth, a UBI would in all likelihood increase the power of organized labour rather than undermining the union movement as some suggest. Individuals would have less to fear from undertaking collective action such as strikes, while potentially having more free time to become involved in union activities. It would also reduce the need for trade unions to spend valuable resources on 'strike funds', allowing more to be spent on policy and strategic development purposes. Finally, and very much related to the point here about the freeing of labour time for non-capitalist forms of collective action, a UBI would provide a massive boost for the diversity of community and social economy activities. Providing a basic income takes away some of the financial risks involved in getting involved with voluntary community activities or starting up new initiatives such as cooperative projects.

Many trade unionists do, however, oppose a UBI, sensing that it might reduce the battle for collective rights in the workplace, although this clearly depends on local context and may reflect their own vested interests – as organizations who ultimately derive their strength from workplace organizing – over a concern for individual economic security. Another criticism made by some social democrats and union leaders is that its prohibitive costs will require massive cutbacks in social provision elsewhere, being a 'Trojan Horse' in effect for new attacks on the distributive aspects of the welfare state by the right. A further concern is that a UBI will increase workfare dependency, leading to falling labour market participation and damaging the economy: 'why would anyone turn up at work anymore if we all get free money?' is a common refrain that we hear both from trade unions and employers. Surely, everyone has the obligation to work for a living.

Such dire predictions around universal income benefits are of course nothing new. But the experience of Nordic countries in the twentieth century tells a different story. Here, the co-existence of high levels of progressive taxation, employment rights, generous welfare entitlements (equating largely to a UBI) and strong trade unions have all persisted alongside high levels of labour productivity, full employment and low levels of inequality, indicating the kind of positive trajectory that might follow the introduction of a UBI. Many of the criticisms lack much empirical foundation. The more authoritative systematic research tends to find little evidence that unemployment rises dramatically or that labour market participation falls overall (Widerquist 2018), although some individuals do take the opportunity to reduce hours for positive reasons such as spending more time with children, family and in volunteering activity. The biggest positives, however, tend to be improvements in the physical and mental health of participants and in the greater likelihood of young people staying on for longer in education.[1]

One way to make the UBI more palatable to mainstream opinion might be to adopt the late Tony Atkinson's term of a 'participation income', whereby recipients are expected to make a 'social contribution' which can be broader than the labour market, including caring for dependents, training or education enrolment (Atkinson 1996). Such a compromise might also invoke an important component of active citizenship to contribute to, and participate in, society.

Critically, the broad argument and point here is that a UBI would enable people to make positive choices regarding work and employment, thereby strengthening their economic rights but only if it runs alongside other legislation and mechanisms to tackle inequality and poverty. These would include policies such as a decent national Living Wage, which in the United States would require a massive increase from the current federal minimum wage of $7.25 to $16.14 (Nadeau and Glasmeier 2019).[2] It would also require a regime with progressive taxation and even a maximum wage[3] to tackle the kinds of massive inequalities that erode the democratic process and produce the conditions leading to the rise of right-wing populism.

Another important element required to strengthen individual economic freedoms is a political agenda to reduce statutory working hours – a movement that had largely stalled due to lack of support among centre left governments since the late 1990s. Not only would this be critical in freeing up time away from work for individual flourishing and diverse choices – to devote to leisure, other forms of creative and fulfilling activity, to spend more time with family life and enhance citizen participation and engagement in the broader community and society – but it would also help to redistribute available paid work in an advanced and more automated economy.[4] Interestingly some recent local experiments to move from a five- to a four-day week in Sweden and New Zealand also suggest considerable productivity benefits for firms, with workers returning more energized by the extra day off (Graham-McLay 2018).

Emergent tendencies in democratic collective ownership

The massive and continued privatizations across the world since the 1970s have been a hallmark of neoliberalism. They have also been a central component in the transfer of resources away from the common good to private wealth accumulation. Despite the claims of its arch proponents, such as the former British Prime Minister Margaret Thatcher, that they wished to create property-owning democracies, mass privatization programmes throughout the world have led to the concentration of ownership rather than its dispersal (see figure 2). In response, there has been a recent upsurge in new forms of democratic collective ownership in both public (state) sectors and cooperative forms.

At the local level, a push back against privatization has been evident for some time.[5] Research by the Transnational Institute has detailed over 800 cases worldwide of towns, cities and regions that have since 2000 taken back into public hands formerly privatized assets, especially in the water and energy sectors, but also transport, waste and cleaning services (Kishimoto and Petitjean 2017). This 'remunicipalization' wave is notable for its geographical reach, although it has been especially prevalent in countries with decentralized governance systems, such as Germany, the United States and France, where local authorities have had the power to terminate or not renew private contracts. Cities as diverse as Berlin, Bordeaux, Cochabamba, Dar es Salaam, Houston and Jakarta have all witnessed successful remunicipalizations. In Mali and Uruguay, national water services themselves have returned to public hands after failed privatization experiments.

Although in the majority of cases, the shift back from privatization has been taken on pragmatic grounds with private solutions failing to deliver affordable public services or the promised improvements and investments in infrastructure, another important motivation has been the desire to re-appropriate local resources and assets to the common good. In Germany, for example, the strong green political pressure to shift towards renewable energy has focused attention on the need for collective and public solutions to tackle climate change, rather than relying on the private sector.[6] There is no doubt too that the process has mobilized citizens and social movements to challenge the status quo and develop alternative, more radical political projects. For example, the remunicipalization campaign in Berlin demanded not just the return of public ownership but a more democratic participatory form of municipal enterprise and a stronger focus on tackling poverty and inequality (Cumbers and Becker 2018).

Remunicipalization has also produced some important innovations in new forms of democratic collective ownership. One example is the small German town of Wolfhagen (population 14,000) in the state of Hessen, which took back its electricity grid from the large private utility Eon (Chakrabortty 2018) in 2006, replacing it with a new public utility where 25 per cent of the shares are held in a specially created local community cooperative. Thirteen years later, the company has doubled its staff, paid off its initial loans, built its own wind turbine and solar panels to achieve 100 per cent locally sourced renewable energy, while using its profits to subsidize local kindergartens.

Other new forms of 'hybrid' local public ownership have developed that mix local state ownership with employee engagement, including the remunicipalized water company in the Greater Buenos Aires region. Here a workers' cooperative holds 10 per cent of the shares, with the trade unions also being instrumental in providing the know-how and skills to run the company after the collapse of the private operator. This has led to both a reduction in costs, compared to the private company, and the opportunity to provide technical advice to other public enterprises across Latin America.[7] Another model of collective ownership was used to build the world's largest offshore wind farm – the Mittelgrunden complex – off the coast of Copenhagen in 2001, a project that meets 3 per cent of the city's electricity needs. Acceptance of the project by the local population was facilitated by the ownership structure with a fifty-fifty split between the local utility company, Copenhagen Energy (itself owned by the city council) and a bespoke cooperative. The latter was created with the aid of the city council's energy department and the support of local residents' groups – in which individuals were able to buy shares, with over 10,000 residents taking up the option (Soerensen et al. 2003).

One interesting recent development to make public enterprises more accountable to citizens has been the setting up of citizen assemblies or roundtables that scrutinize their work. Many cities in France have established such forms of citizen engagement alongside the remunicipalization of water services. Paris, for example, has set up a Water Observatory – a citizens' forum that has access to all company operations and documents – that can hold the local public water company to account and has a directly elected representative on the board. The city of Montpellier has gone even further with 30 per cent of its new board elected by local residents.

An interesting example of a hybrid form of democratic collective ownership at the national level comes from Costa Rica, where the country's third largest bank, the Banco Popular y de Desarrollo Comunal (BPDC) – which translates as the Popular Bank for Community Development – was set up as a public bank but under the legal ownership of the country's workers in 1969 (Marois 2017). To own a share in the bank, a worker needs to have had a savings account with the bank for one year. The most recent figures suggest that the bank has 1.2 million members or 20 per cent of the total population. The key governing body of the bank is a democratic assembly of 290 representatives elected from different economic and social sectors among the bank's member owners, whilst the main operational board, the National Board of Directors, is composed of seven members, four from the assembly and three from government with at least 50 per cent women (currently four out of seven). Twenty-five per cent of the bank's revenues go to fund social projects, and it has played an increasingly important role in the country's rapid expansion of renewable energy, including a partnering with the rural energy cooperative COOPELESCA to help finance its post-carbon transition, becoming the first Latin American energy supplier to become carbon neutral in 2013 (Marois 2017).

Beyond these examples, two cases are worth exploring in more depth here to illustrate how larger scale innovations in democratic collective ownership are achievable and the positive social and ecological outcomes that they can produce: Denmark's collectively owned revolution in renewable energy and the Mondragon employee ownership network in the Basque Region.

Denmark's collectively owned renewables revolution

While Denmark is rightly held up as a role model in its transformation from one of the most oil-dependent countries in the world in the 1970s to a global leader in renewable energy, rather less well known is the role of democratic collective ownership and public participation in this story. Following an effective grassroots campaign to change the direction of energy policy in the 1970s (see Cumbers 2012: chapter 9, for more details), supportive government policies in the 1980s such as investment subsidies, feed-in tariffs and energy efficiency measures helped to boost the growth of renewables (especially wind power).

Local ownership laws that required owners of wind turbines to be resident locally had the effect of encouraging the formation of cooperatives, in a country with a strong mutualist tradition, so that by the late 1990s, around 150,000 families, or around

10 per cent of the population, were involved in the ownership of wind turbines, with 80 per cent of these in cooperatives or family ownership (Cumbers 2012). Because the electricity and heating systems have remained under local municipal public ownership, as are the regional distribution networks (all of which have democratically elected boards), although the grid remains in national state ownership, it has been easier for Denmark to develop integrated policies to shift decisively towards non-carbon district heating systems while modernizing the grid to allow better connectivity for its decentralized wind power sector.

A further effect of the high level of public participation in the energy transition has been the emergence of collective associations such as the Danish Wind Turbine Owners Association (DWTOA), the Danish Wind Industry Association and the Nordic Folkecenter for Renewable Energy. The latter has become an influential and well-regarded non-profit body campaigning for new and efficient non-carbon technologies on the international stage. Surrounding these organizations, a strong active and knowledgeable energy civil society of green think tanks, academics and environmental groups has emerged to decisively shift energy policy (and construct a strong national consensus) away from carbon and nuclear towards renewable energy in all its diverse forms.

Mondragon's employee-owned enterprise network
The much-discussed Mondragon network of worker cooperatives in the Basque Region in Spain remains inspirational for many because of its ability to adapt and innovate – as well as any private corporation – in the face of challenging global economic circumstances. Currently employing around 74,000 workers globally across over 100 different cooperatives in a diverse range of industrial and services sectors, Mondragon is committed to the basic principle of 'labour sovereignty' (Heales et al. 2017: 13) and is viewed as 'a relatively pure form of democratic worker ownership' (Ellerman 1990: 95). Workers in every cooperative have an annual General Assembly, which on the basis of one member, one vote approves the business plan and budget, as well as electing a Governing Council (the board of directors) and an audit committee. Another key democratic institution is an elected Social Council that has discussions with management regarding working conditions and other issues.

Much of its success in growing and adapting in difficult economic times relates to its emphasis on innovation and training with its own educational and technology institutes. One authoritative study (Arando et al. 2011) has suggested that its deep commitment to democracy is a key ingredient in its success, including successfully weathering the financial crisis, also relating to having its own bank to provide financial independence. Its democratic decision-making processes have also fostered a high degree of intra-network cooperation, collective knowledge sharing and an emphasis on lifelong learning alongside job security. In short, measures of public effectiveness and social values that contrast strongly with the profit maximization mantra of privately-owned firms.

Part of the wider appeal of Mondragon is the speed at which it has developed – since its founding in 1956 with 25 employee members – to an entire regional ecosystem of worker cooperatives by the 1990s. This suggests the possibilities for scaling up cooperative ownership forms to the local and perhaps even national economy through supportive state policies around ownership rules (note also the Danish experience above), public procurement initiatives and government support. It has recently been the inspiration for a number of community wealth-building initiatives in a range of places from Cleveland in the US to Preston in the UK (Guinan and O'Neill 2019).

Practising participatory economic decision making

As should by now be evident, increased public involvement and more collective deliberation of decision making are not only crucial for economic democracy, but they can also enhance the effectiveness of the economy through stimulating collective learning processes. In other words, the bringing together of diverse forms of knowledge to inform economic decision making. While I have already discussed examples of this within the workplace at Lucas (in chapter 2) and Mondragon, there are also some important experiments in citizen participation in wider economic practice that we can draw upon. Here, I will catalogue a few of the most interesting and significant initiatives.

One of the most well-known is participatory budgeting (PB), where governments devote a proportion of their budget directly to citizens' groups who are brought together in a series of deliberative exercises to decide on investment priorities. PB was first introduced in the southern Brazilian city of Porto Alegre following the victory of the Workers Party in local elections in 1988. Regional assemblies of residents were set up across the city to vote on priorities, which were then fed into city-level planning processes. A surprisingly positive (given the institution's dominant neoliberal discourse) World Bank study in the early 2000s reported on the significant improvements that had occurred in the city after a decade of PB operations. According to its report, PB had stimulated improvements in everything from the city's water and sanitation services, children's school enrolment and investment in transport infrastructure (World Bank 2003). PB has spread throughout Brazil with over 120 cities adopting PBs in the 1990s and 2000s and more widely across the world. There are currently over 250 schemes in the US, with Chicago and New York being important centres.[8]

It remains, however, a relatively marginal phenomenon. In Brazil, cities typically allocate between 5 and 15 per cent of the total budget. Nevertheless, its advocates point to some important impacts, particularly in increasing the participation of women and lower income groups in democratic processes. Where it is sustained over a longer time period, there is evidence that it reduces corruption, improves transparency and public engagement and creates better institutions that incorporate citizens' voices more regularly into governance processes. The Brazilian evidence also suggests that it leads to greater spending on health and education in poorer areas of cities with a significant impact in reducing infant mortality, while also linked to the growth of civil society organizations (Gonçalves 2014; Touchton and Wampler 2014).

The City of Melbourne carried out an interesting variant of PB in 2014 when it set up a 'People's Panel' as part of the development of its ten-year financial plan, involving $5 billion of total spending. The panel was part of a broader participatory process that involved online consultations, including a budget simulator, encouragement for citizens to consider economic trade-offs between competing options and pop-up policy booths across the city.[9] The panel represented a diverse 'mini-public' of 43 people drawn from across the city, although business people occupied more than half of the places and the budget agreed was fairly fiscally conservative. Nevertheless, there were some relatively progressive decisions, including some debt financing for investment and increased funding for environmental and sustainability measures to tackle climate change. Eleven recommendations were made, all of which were included in the final city plan.

Going beyond these local experiments, there have been calls to make higher level macroeconomic decision making open to greater public scrutiny, accountability and participation. One innovative project run by the UK's Royal Society for the Arts (RSA) put together a Citizen's Economic Council (Patel and Gibbon 2017: 11), which brought citizens – particularly from economically 'left behind' regions of the country – to deliberate with a diverse range of experts and organizations on key economic problems as well as on different alternative policies. Among its recommendations was the need for much better 'jargon-free' communication about the economy by expert groups and government bodies as a way of drawing citizens into the economic policy debate. Another set of interesting recommendations is for citizens panels to inform macroeconomic decision bodies, such as the setting of interest rates, an idea that received some support from the Bank of England Chief Economist Andrew Haldane who has initiated his own series of Town Hall 'listening events'.[10]

Elsewhere, there have been some important initiatives to embed economic decision making into broader democratic practice. This has included the setting up of a Constitutional Convention in Ireland (of 100 people, two-thirds randomly selected from the electoral register and one-third from political parties) to inform the modification of the country's constitution in 2014. Among its recommendations were a greater commitment to gender equality and women's access to the workplace, which is under consideration by government, and the more radical proposal – not adopted despite 85 per cent of the convention supporting it (TCOTC 2014) – to strengthen basic economic and social rights. The Convention has been an interesting exercise in public deliberation, open to both submissions from the public on the eight topics selected, as well as being advised by academic and legal experts and advocacy groups. Like many other countries, Ireland's constitution also permits a certain amount of direct democracy through referenda, a famous recent outcome being the vote to allow abortions for the first time in 2018. This followed an earlier Citizens Assembly on the subject that prepared much of the ground work. The Assembly – a similar body of 100 people to the Convention – also debated how to strengthen climate change policy and prepare for an ageing society.

A final example comes from Iceland where, following the financial crisis in 2008, the Parliament decided to completely revise the country's constitution (see Patel and Gibbon 2017: 17–19). In 2012 a Constitutional Council of 25 elected citizens – from 522 people who stood in the special elections – was established. These included some existing politicians and public figures (such as a trade union leader) alongside ordinary citizens. The Council was given the remit to construct a new constitution based on the recommendations from an earlier National Assembly of 950 randomly selected citizens. Of the provisions put forward for voting on by the public, the one that received most support (83 per cent in favour) was that Iceland's remaining natural resources not in private hands (including control over controversial fishing rights) should be placed firmly under democratic public ownership and control. Other provisions in the Bill were designed to guarantee basic social welfare rights, provision of internet access for every citizen, and to increase accountability and freedom of information in business and public sectors. In the words of one elected councillor, the concern was in: 'breaking a pervasive culture of secrecy that has enabled the political class to get away with, among other things, the Russian-style privatization of the banks in the period from 1998–2003 that paved the way off the edge of cliff in 2008' (Gylfason 2012).

Sadly, subsequent events have reinforced this cynicism about the political class. Despite massive majority support for the proposals, the return of a centre right government in 2013 – with links to business and fishing interests – has so far obstructed the implementation of the constitution with some political figures that were originally supportive rowing back against earlier commitments. The government somewhat derisorily reduced the status of the constitution to an 'irrelevant opinion poll' (Gylfason 2014).

Conclusion

Summarizing these diverse experiences, there are some important general lessons to draw out. Significantly, in all three pillars of economic democracy, there remains considerable opposition to the proposed innovations, especially from dominant vested interests who would see their powers and control of the economy greatly weakened. There is also substantial opposition from some more progressive quarters for innovative proposals such as the UBI, which are variously attacked as either too expensive or impractical. However, whether it is the UBI or participatory budgeting, or developing more democratic engagement in new forms of collective ownership, the evidence suggests that democracy also comes with improvements in outcomes, often in organizational performance but particularly in addressing key social and ecological priorities.

Particularly troubling is the way that mainstream political parties and established interests (of centre left and right) seek to block what are often overwhelming publicly mandated democratic preferences and decisions. In the case of Iceland, as Thorvaldur Gylfason, the former council member and Professor of Economics at the University of Iceland, succinctly puts it: 'the most democratic constitution bill ever drafted is being held hostage by self-serving politicians in the clearest possible demonstration of a fundamental principle of constitution-making – namely, that politicians should neither be tasked with drafting nor ratifying constitutions because of the risk that they will act against the public interest' (Gylfason 2014).

Clearly, such setbacks show that there are considerable obstacles that democratic initiatives face in circumventing established political and business elites. Yet as the RSA rightly warns in its report, such duplicitous short termism on behalf of politicians against participatory and deliberative processes leads to even greater public disenchantment with politics and potentially democracy itself. The most significant pushback from established elites comes when individual economic rights are advocated in a radical way that infringes upon employer and corporate rights to manage and control labour and work, or when the broader ownership and property rights of private enterprise are under threat. Yet, taking aim at the elite control of work, resources and the ownership of our economy is precisely the battle that must be fought for economic democracy.

More positively, what is also clear is that where citizens come together in deliberative settings, with a diverse range of experts, knowledge and experience, and where they have the time and resources to engage in policy details, they do produce progressive social and ecological strategies that are, more often than not, far in advance of what political parties are willing to contemplate. It is striking also that such deliberations come to firm conclusions about both the importance of individual economic and social rights and the importance of securing public goods and assets for the common good.

Conclusion

Constructing the democratic economy

My aim in this book has been to offer some insights into how we can rethink economic democracy for the twenty-first century. Like others (e.g. Schweickart 2002; Alperovitz 2005; Blackburn 2007; Malleson 2013; Solimano 2014), this is founded upon my belief that solving the world's political, social and ecological crises requires a transformation away from a rapacious neoliberal capitalism towards a democratic economy. Where my emphasis in the book is different is in envisaging it as a project of both securing individual economic rights as well as enhancing and developing collective solutions.[1]

This involves a slight recalibration, extending the current focus on collective bargaining in the workplace or encouraging cooperative and employee ownership, to include also a discussion of individual self-governance and what this requires. At a basic level, this involves the resources and skills for every individual, regardless of gender, skin colour, class position and religious affiliation, to lead functioning and meaningful lives of their own choosing. For me, this question is not mutually exclusive from a collective class project for social justice but must run alongside it, recognizing that work and economic activity more broadly are always cooperative ventures.

Individual well-being is inextricably tied up with the broader common wealth, a sentiment shared in their very different world views by communists such as Karl Marx, or liberals like Adam Smith and John Stuart Mill. We do not, and cannot, exist outside of a broader community and society, whatever the imaginative delusions of neoliberals. The rhetorical capture of the individual – as an atomized and selfish actor – and its welding to the rights to hold property and control the labour of others, when implemented in such force by global elites in the past forty years, produces massive wealth appropriation, inequality and ecological destruction. We need to remind ourselves that the individual is inextricably part of the collective and therefore that a fully functioning democracy must uphold individual rights but in ways that admit broader social responsibilities. The three pillars of economic democracy that I have advanced here are an attempt to tie the individual and the collective together through democratic processes.

A summary of the main arguments and their policy implications

Enshrining a set of basic individual economic rights is the fundamental starting point for economic democracy. As I have argued throughout the book, many on the left – with their focus around a collective class interest – lost sight of the importance of the individual, often at the expense of a commitment to universal economic, social and political rights. Yet, freeing the individual from oppressive servitude of both their labour under capitalism and enabling them to make meaningful and flourishing life choices was surely the core motivation behind Marx's whole canon of radical political economy.[2] Its neglect can lead to the marginalization of particular social groups on the basis of race, gender and class, as I alluded to in chapter 1, as well as to the kinds of totalitarian politics that stained the last century and led to Nazism and genocide. As a response to this experience, economic democracy needs to be framed within a broader narrative and aspiration to universalism, explicit in the 1948 UN Universal Declaration of Human Rights which among other things commits itself to securing the 'life, liberty and security of person' (Article 3) as well as strong rights to decent employment, free of servitude, and to 'a standard of living adequate for ... health and well-being' (UN 1948: Article 25).

Taking individual economic rights seriously contains three essential elements or pillars (table 3). First, the rights to self-government of one's own labour takes precedence over the property rights of firms to own and control the labour of others. This self-government of labour can then be extended beyond the capitalist workplace to autonomy over work in all spheres of life, which in turn means the ability to access the resources to make meaningful choices to lead a flourishing life. There are a range of diverse but already existing institutional mechanisms that can – if delivered in full as a package of policies – construct this pillar: a system of progressive taxation that is able to fully redistribute income and wealth to overcome the inequality of opportunity that underpins capitalism and enables massive appropriation by elites; strong legislation around equal rights and access to education, employment and constitutional protection, irrespective of gender, race or other socio-cultural attributes; the replacement of the post-war system of welfare dependency with one that articulates a set of more enabling economic and social rights, such as a universal basic income and universal service access; and finally, minimum wage levels set at the level of an affordable living wage for an individual and their dependants.

The individual, however, is inextricably a part of the collective: the 'I' becomes the 'we' once we accept the idea of the social, rather than the selfish, individual. Labour and economic activity are always at some basic level collective projects as part of broader society. Individual rights must always be in negotiation and collaboration with others. Hence, a democratic economy involves a shift away from the current private and hierarchical corporate organizational forms, where elite groups and individuals have proprietorial property rights over the labour of others, towards a mixed economy of collective ownership, which is the second fundamental pillar for economic democracy, as outlined at length in chapter 2.

To summarize my argument here, greater democratization needs a radical shift towards diverse forms

Table 3. The Pillars of Economic Democracy: Essential Elements and Institutional Mechanisms

Pillar	Essential elements	Institutional mechanisms
Individual economic rights	– Rights of labour versus property rights – Self-government of labour in and beyond the workplace – Resources and skills for flourishing + 'choiceworthy' lives	– System of progressive income, wealth and land taxation – Strong equal rights legislation including constitutional economic and social rights – Replacement of dependent welfare state with universal and comprehensive rights entitlement – Minimum wages at a level of a living wage
Diverse forms of collective ownership	– Collective 'appropriation rights' over the social surplus – Construction of the common good versus elite vested interests – Reinvigorate democratic state planning	– Legal regulation to secure collective provision of essential goods and services – Mixed economy of state + non-state collective ownership – Re-regulation of markets and finance for the common good

| Creating deliberative and knowledgeable publics | – Rights for collective action
– Active and contested civil society
– Principles of pluralism, diverse and competing perspectives | – Legal reductions in working time to permit citizen participation
– Strengthening of collective bargaining
– State support for political parties and associated research foundations
– Democratization of macroeconomic governance
– Greater accountability, transparency and regulation of international organizations and corporations
– International tax arrangements to tackle multinational corporate spatial dexterity |

of collective public ownership (both state and non-state) which are able to articulate the common good in opposition to private and increasingly financialized wealth appropriation. And, as the Mondragon model of worker cooperatives demonstrates, there is the possibility of creating local ecosystems of collective democratic ownership that are 'a plausible stepping stone towards economic democracy' (Blackburn 2007: 41) and away from an economy dominated by global corporate organizations and massive inequalities in wealth. The experience of Denmark with its renewables revolution, and the Costa Rican Banco Popular example, also illustrate the extent to which democratic collective forms of ownership do prioritize social over narrow commercial and economic targets.

This brings us to the third pillar, and perhaps the most difficult aspect to legislate for, given that creating deliberative and knowledgeable publics – in other words seeding a thriving active democratic culture around economic decision making – is less of a tangible outcome than a process that can take different forms. Nevertheless, there are three essential elements, as laid out in previous chapters: rights to collective action, an active but also contested and politicized civil society,[3] and, following Mouffe (2000), a political culture of 'agonistic pluralism', tolerant of competing perspectives, yet not one which reduces them to a faux consensus.

There are important ingredients that already exist in different places that seem important to encouraging pluralism and deliberative politics in the economic realm. The German state funding of political foundations is interesting in this respect and could be a model emulated elsewhere. It has enabled the left-wing foundation, the Rosa Luxemburg Stiftung, to become an important global advocate for energy democracy and more radical approaches to participatory democracy. The Heinrich Böll Foundation has been a similarly important initiative in promoting more radical green agendas domestically and internationally. Germany also has its own trade union research foundation, the Hans-Böckler-Foundation, partly established in line with co-determination procedures, but also able to provide its own well-respected expertise in economic policy, including setting up its own Macroeconomic Policy Institute in 2005. While there is always the tension and danger of such institutions being incorporated into more conservative state agendas, as is all too evident with many German social democratic and labour organizations, they remain important institutions for maintaining pluralism and alternative economic narratives.

Conclusion

A further element critical to both first and third pillars would be legislation to reduce working time, and the campaign for a four-day week is an important initiative in this respect. Higher wage levels and a UBI would work alongside this provision to provide individuals with more free time, some of which would enable much greater citizen engagement in economic decision-making activity, time for training and education and the development of skills to become 'lay experts', able to participate on more equal terms with professional and technically qualified personnel. The ability to become members of cooperative boards or democratic assemblies is severely restricted at present, particularly for lower income groups working long hours in two or three jobs just to make ends meet. Greater free time would also enable fuller democratic macroeconomic governance of key institutions such as central banks and other key state and quasi-state institutions.

Alongside these three pillars – which are focused at the national level – there is clearly a need for mechanisms and policies at the global level that could tackle the power of corporations (not least their ability to lobby and pressurize governments and international institutions), the hyper-globalization of financial markets, nefarious labour practices and corporate tax avoidance strategies. Although this is a daunting task, the architecture does potentially exist through current global governance institutions. But it would require very different political actors and forces running things in the most powerful nation states and regional economic blocs such as the European Union than we have at present. There are some important international initiatives that provide hope in the form of international labour campaigns, fair-trade networks, variants of the Tobin tax[4] and a more recent initiative by ICRICT (the Independent Commission for the Reform of International Corporate Taxation) to propose a global minimum effective corporate tax rate. These initiatives, together with more redistribution of wealth between the Global North and South, would be needed to enable poorer developing economies to create forms of economic democracy on their own terms.

Mobilizing for economic democracy

During public discussion of the ideas outlined here, one of the toughest questions that comes back from the audience is: ok, this all sounds great but how do we get there? Highlighting actually existing examples, such as that of the Danish renewables experience and a realistic assessment of their achievements and the transferable lessons, is one (albeit limited) response. But, beyond such individual success stories, large powerful multinational organizations, the financial and political elite (the dominant vested interests of our time) are not going to submit quietly. There are some who argue that these interests can be assuaged through a kinder or softer version of capitalism (Hay and Payne 2015). But this seems to me far too naïve, given our political-economic trajectory, which seems set to accelerate inequality and ecological damage rather than moderate them. Contemporary global capitalism, with its focus around destructive growth, rapacious competition and the internal dynamic of profit-centred economic development, seems the very antithesis of the collectively organized democratic economy framed around social and ecological justice that we surely need. So, how can we transform our economy in the way envisaged here? And what kinds of political and social forces would be required?

Too often the state becomes a reactionary filter for arresting and draining democratic movements and collective action, as the experience of Iceland in the last chapter attests. Spontaneous and grassroots uprisings and rebellions against the status quo are quelled, and alternative egalitarian proposals – arrived at through deliberative, participatory and negotiated collective practices – are modified, diluted or abandoned altogether through the vested elite interests and bureaucratic conservatism of state organs and institutions. For this reason, many on the left – particularly in the anarchist, libertarian socialist and autonomous communist traditions – are rightly suspicious of any project for economic democracy that focuses upon the formal organizations and apparatus of the state, political parties, state recognized trade unions and so on.

My own approach to economic democracy resonates strongly with the political agenda around forging a new global commons; where we free ourselves from the oppressive institutions of capitalism and top-down bureaucratic state management to create new institutions and organizations for collective self-governance (Holloway 2010; De Angelis 2016). However, tackling the three most important crises facing us – climate change, economic inequality and the crisis of democracy – require complex multi-layered and multi-scalar solutions that cannot wish away the state, however problematic it is in its current form. A project for a radical anti-capitalist economic democracy must therefore seek to work through and reclaim the state (Wainwright 2003), while continuing to foment new autonomous spaces outside it. This would require working with those in existing left and green political parties that share the aspiration to build a more democratic and egalitarian economy, whether this is labelled anti-capitalist or not, and recognizing the difficulties of becoming incorporated into existing elite projects and overcoming complicit trade union and social democratic actors.

Given that the project of economic democracy is one of individual and collective self-governance of labour, the trade union movement remains a crucial political actor for securing the kinds of changes desired here. State institutions, left political parties, along with trade unions themselves, need massive reform and deep democratization – so that they also become true institutions of radical self-governance from below – rather than top-down instruments of elite control. If we succeed, these will look very different to what we have now. As Hilary Wainwright puts it so eloquently – in an exchange with John Holloway:

In the forms of organisation and – I insist – self-determined institutions that we create to resist alienation in all its forms, aren't we aiming to pre-figure in our own organisations a different kind of citizenship? A citizenship where when we elect people (and we will need forms of both representation and delegation) who don't then turn that very power we lent them back against us – who won't, in other words, present politics as an alienated form. (Wainwright and Holloway 2011)

Many of the institutions to secure individual and collective rights can only be constructed through some type of state apparatus, but this can be a radically different kind of citizen state to either the bureaucratic welfare state or the neoliberal state (Wainwright 2003).

The project against elite co-option will always be a continuing struggle – and need ongoing renewal and new configurations – as conditions in our global political economy change, a reality recognized by the more pragmatic anti-capitalists and socialists (Wright 2011). Whatever the limits of Nordic social democracy, it is worth remembering that, as represented in the Meidner Plan, it forged one of the most radical proposals for the transfer of ownership from capital to labour yet conceived. This was because it combined strong achievements at state level with collective trade union strength, itself forged by earlier workplace struggles, fusing with new social mobilizations to push democratic collective ownership and governance a stage further.

In our own time, resurgent left projects on both sides of the Atlantic – together with the myriad local municipal coalitions bringing together older and newer forms of social movement around radical projects for social and ecological justice – demonstrate the art of the politically possible as well as the constraints and blockages from established vested interests. The key lesson to take from earlier struggles for economic democracy in the twentieth century is the importance of mass mobilization, an organized labour movement as part of a diverse coalition of social forces, and an alternative economic vision to strive for, that can also 'name the enemy' and confront it. Whether the Green New Deal as currently being espoused can be this vision remains to be seen. But hopefully a version of it, especially a radical one linked to a renewed call for a democratic and egalitarian economy, might fit the bill.

The good news is that the form of neoliberalized global capitalism that currently exploits and alienates both us and the natural environment has never been less popular. The distaste for the financial class since the 2008–9 crisis remains while there is a growing awareness of the multiple failings of the wider economic system. The popularity of the UK Labour Party's economic democracy agenda, as evoked in its Alternative Models of Ownership report (Labour Party 2017) at the 2017 General Election, clearly took many political and business elites by surprise. In the wake of that election, an opinion poll commissioned by the right-wing Legatum Institute found incredibly strong support among the public for the return of privatized industries to public ownership: 83 per cent for water, 77 per cent for electricity and gas and 76 per cent for train services. Fifty per cent also wanted to bring the banking sector into public ownership, suggesting a ready audience for Labour's imaginative proposals for a new 'public banking ecosystem' (Berry and Macfarlane 2019). These are remarkable figures given the dominance of capitalist economic values in the country's mainstream media and the absence of alternative perspectives in everyday public debate.

Our twenty-first-century struggle for economic democracy must be one that strives for a transition away from fossil fuels, from financialized, deregulatory neoliberal capitalism towards the democratic economy that can tackle existing social and ecological injustices. Happily, the public mood is increasingly demanding a more radical collective

Conclusion

response to the problems we face, which will at the same time mean taking on and defeating the vested interests that continue to undermine our common wealth. As is evident from some of the policies and proposals discussed here, and the growing tide of protest among ordinary citizens, an alternative democratic economy is within our grasp. But to produce sustainable solutions to the crises we face, I have argued strongly here for a project that enables individual economic rights and ambitions alongside collective ownership and radical democracy.

Notes

Introduction

1 See, for example, senior Democrat Nancy Pelosi's recent dismissal of the Green New Deal in the US.
2 Some research that I carried out for the Scottish public sector union, UNISON, in the mid-2000s showed no significant relationship between level of taxation and economic growth when comparing countries in the OECD (Birch and Cumbers 2007).

Chapter 1 A Brief History of Economic Democracy as Industrial Democracy

1 See Geoff Mann's excellent recent articulation of this perspective on Keynes and other liberals (Mann 2017).
2 David Harvey (2003), drawing on Rosa Luxemburg (1968), usefully distinguishes between 'accumulation by dispossession' and 'intensive accumulation' in

identifying these twin appropriative and exploitative dynamics of capitalism.

3 I should say from the outset that my history is restricted to the period since the industrial revolution and has a Western-centric bias, recognizing that there are many earlier and even continuing forms of more democratically organized collective economies than the current dominant model of global capitalism.

4 There are some interesting exceptions, for example Denmark, where a much more decentralized, associational model of capitalism developed in which cooperatives played a very strong role (Cumbers 2012: chapter 9). Many unions and labour movements also favoured and worked with cooperative associations and even established their own, as part of their struggles to improve the conditions of their members. The German trade union movement, the DGB, for example, had a strong commitment to a cooperative economy as an alternative to capitalism from the 1920s onwards (Müller-Jentsch 2018).

5 These issues are discussed in greater depth in Cumbers (2012: chapter 1).

6 See Müller-Jentsch (2018) for a critical longer term perspective.

7 See Guinan (2019) for a recent critical review.

8 See Meidner's own reflections on the plan (Meidner 1993).

9 See Cumbers (2012).

10 After Friedrich Von Hayek, Thatcher's favourite

proponent of free market philosophy and private enterprise.

11 See, for example, Featherstone (2012).

12 The extent of patriarchy in the post-1945 welfare regimes that emerged in Western Europe varied between a 'weaker male breadwinner model' in Sweden to stronger versions in countries such as the UK and Ireland, for example, where married women were prevented from working in the civil service until 1977 (Lewis 1992).

Chapter 2 The Three Pillars of Economic Democracy

1 Where it was less effective was in adjusting to the more difficult economic circumstances of the late 1970s and 1980s, particularly rising oil prices, but arguably this had more to do with the lack of a co-ordinated national macroeconomic strategy than with the self-managed enterprise model (Estrin 1991).

2 I have written elsewhere on the limits of market socialism (e.g. Cumbers 2012: chapter 3).

3 I have developed arguments for diverse and multi-stakeholder forms of public ownership in greater depth in Cumbers (2012: chapter 7) and in an updated form in Cumbers (2017).

4 See the important arguments for a very different economics of care in health services in Davis and McMaster (2017).

5 The proposals are elaborated on in greater depth in Cumbers (2012: chapter 7) and Cumbers (2017).

6 An excellent recent discussion of the impact of these practices in the retail sector is provided by Kerevan (2019).

7 See Fine and Saad-Filho (2014) for a useful recent summary and discussion.

Chapter 3 Putting Economic Democracy into Practice

1 See Widerquist (2018) for a comprehensive and relatively balanced summary of the benefits and problems.

2 In the UK this would require a shift from the current minimum wage of £7.30 to £9, and £10.55 in London.

3 See arguments set out for a maximum wage in Ramsay (2005).

4 See Gorz (1999: chapter 4).

5 See, for example, a recent report by the right-wing Legatum Institute (Elliott and Kanagasooriam, 2017).

6 The investment required for infrastructure improvements to meet Germany's renewable energy targets could be up to €42 billion alone.

7 One example is a partnership with the Peruvian city, Huancayo, to modernize its sanitation services in the face of pressures to privatize it in return for funding from international investors and the World Bank.

8 Further information on North American PB experiences is available at: https://www.participatorybudgeting.org/impacts/. See also the excellent review in Menser (2018).

9 This and other participatory experiments are reported

on in the RSA's excellent research project on citizen economic councils. For further information on this excellent initiative and its recommendations, see Patel and Gibbon (2017).

10 See his speech on 'Everyday Economics', delivered at a school in Birmingham on 27 November 2017: https://www.bankofengland.co.uk/-/media/boe/files/s peech/2017/everyday-economics.pdf?la=en&hash=F 52775115FABD0AA5EA38DE2E0A26CAFD9602 72C.

Conclusion

1 Although see Martin O'Neill's important contribution to rethinking economic democracy from a Rawlsian justice perspective (O'Neill 2008).

2 See Allan Megill's basic argument on this point (Megill 2002). From a slightly different perspective, I think this is an essential element of the thinking of autonomous Marxist writers such as Harry Cleaver and John Holloway.

3 I am influenced here by the Latin American perspective which is to see civil society not in the kinds of mild de-politicized NGO spaces of neoliberal governance but as 'political society' that maintains critical engagement with the state, institutions and political actors that operate through it. See, for example, Dinerstein's discussion of the social and solidarity economy (Dinerstein 2017).

4 The Tobin tax is an international tax on financial transactions originally proposed by James Tobin,

the Nobel Prize-winning economist in the 1970s as a way of throwing 'sand in the wheels' of currency speculation. Originally, it was suggested that as small amount as 0.1 per cent could raise considerable sums to pay for social and economic development and force speculators to moderate their activities. It is once again growing in popularity since the financial crisis with the European Commission, France and Germany particularly keen on developing an international mechanism to tax and regulate speculation.

References

Alperovitz, G. (2005) *America Beyond Capitalism: Reclaiming Our Wealth, Our Liberty and Our Democracy*. Hoboken, NJ: Wiley.

Alvaredo, F., Chancel, L., Piketty, T., Saez, E. and Zucman, G. (2017) *World Inequality Report 2018*. World Inequality Lab, available at: https://wir2018.wid.world

Arando, S., Freundlich, F., Gago, M., Jones, D.C. and Kato, T. (2011) Assessing Mondragon: Stability and managed change in the face of globalization. In E.J. Carberry (ed.) *Employee Ownership and Shared Capitalism: New Directions in Research*. Champaign, IL: Labor and Employment Relations Association and ILR Press.

Atkinson, A.B. (1996) The case for a participation income. *The Political Quarterly*, 67 (1), 67–70.

Avent, R. (2016) Welcome to a world without work. *The Observer*, 9 October.

129

References

Berry, C. and Macfarlane, L. (2019) *A New Public Banking Ecosystem*; a report to the Labour Party commissioned by the Communication Workers Union and the Democracy Collaborative, Labour Party, London.

Birch, K. and Cumbers, A. (2007) Public sector spending and the Scottish economy: crowding out or adding value? *Scottish Affairs*, 58, 36–56.

Blackburn, R. (2007) Economic democracy: Meaningful, desirable, feasible? *Daedalus*, 136 (3), 36–45.

Blyth, M. (2013) *Austerity: The History of a Dangerous Idea*. Oxford: Oxford University Press.

Bonoli, G. (2010) The political economy of active labor-market policy. *Politics & Society*, 38 (4), 435–57.

Brown, W. (2015) *Undoing the Demos: Neoliberalism's Stealth Revolution*. New York: Zone Books.

Burczak, T.A. (2006) *Socialism After Hayek*. Ann Arbor, MI: University of Michigan Press.

Castles, S. (2006) Guestworkers in Europe: a resurrection? *International Migration Review*, 40 (4), 741–66.

Chakraborrty, A. (2018) How a small town reclaimed its grid and sparked a community revolution. *The Guardian*, 28 February.

Cole, G.D.H. (1920) *Guild Socialism Restated*. London: Leonard Parsons.

Crouch, C. (2004) *Post-Democracy*. Cambridge: Polity.

Cumbers, A. (2012) *Reclaiming Public Ownership: Making Space for Economic Democracy*. London: Zed Books.

References

Cumbers, A. (2017) *Diversifying Public Ownership: Constructing Institutions for Participation, Social Empowerment and Democratic Control.* Next System Project, available at: https://thenextsystem.org/ diversifying-public-ownership

Cumbers, A. (2019) A tale of two nationalisations: experiences of post 1945 public ownership in the UK and France compared. *International Journal of Public Policy*, 15 (1–2), 5–20.

Cumbers, A. and Becker, S. (2018) Making sense of remunicipalisation: theoretical reflections on and political possibilities from Germany's Rekommualisierung process. *Cambridge Journal of Regions, Economy and Society*, 11, 503–17.

Dahl, R. (1985) *A Preface to Economic Democracy.* Oakland, CA: University of California Press.

Davis, J.B. and McMaster, R. (2017) *Health Care Economics.* London: Routledge.

De Angelis, M. (2016) *Omnia Sunt Communia: On the Commons and the Transformation to Post-capitalism.* London: Zed Books.

De Martino, G. (2000) *Global Economy, Global Justice.* London: Routledge.

Dinerstein, A. (2017) Co-construction or prefiguration? The problem of the 'translation' of social and solidarity economy practices into policy. In P. North and M.S. Cato (eds) *Towards Just and Sustainable Economies:*

References

The Social and Solidarity Economy North and South. Bristol: Policy Press.

Donovan, S.H. and Bradley, D.H. (2018) *Real Wage Trends: 1979–2017.* Washington, DC: Congressional Research Service.

EIU (2017) *Democracy Index 2017: Free Speech Under Attack.* London: Economist Intelligence Unit.

Ellerman, D. (1990) *The Democratic Worker-Owned Firm.* Boston, MA: Unwin Hyman.

Ellerman, D. (1992) *Property and Contract in Economics: The Case for Economic Democracy.* Oxford: Blackwell Publishing.

Elliott, L. (2019) World's 26 richest people own as much as poorest 50%, says Oxfam. *The Guardian*, 21 January.

Elliott, M. and Kanagasooriam, J. (2017) *Public Opinion in the Post-Brexit Era: Economic Attitudes in Modern Britain.* London: Legatum Institute.

Estrin, S. (1991) Yugoslavia: the case of self-managed market socialism. *Journal of Economic Perspectives*, 5 (4), 187–94.

Featherstone, D. (2012) *Solidarity: Hidden Histories and Geographies of Internationalism.* London: Zed Books.

Featherstone, D. (2019) Maritime labour, transnational political trajectories and decolonization from below: the opposition to the 1935 British Shipping Assistance Act. *Global Networks*, available at: https://doi.org/10.1111/glob.12228

References

Fine, Ben and Saad-Filho, A. (2014) Politics of neoliberal development: Washington Consensus and post-Washington Consensus. In H. Weber (ed.), *The Politics of Development: A Survey*. London: Routledge, pp. 154–66.

Fishman, N. (1993) Coal: owned and managed on behalf of the people. In J. Fyrth (ed.), *Labour's High Noon: The Government and the Economy 1945–51*. London: Lawrence and Wishart.

Fung, A. (2004) *Empowered Participation: Reinventing Urban Democracy*. Princeton, NJ: Princeton University Press.

Gonçalves, S. (2014) The effects of participatory budgeting on municipal expenditures and infant mortality in Brazil. *World Development*, 53, 94–110.

Gorz, A. (1999) *Reclaiming Work: Beyond the Wage-based Society*. Cambridge: Polity.

Gowan, P. (2019) Right to own: a policy framework to catalyze worker ownership transitions. *Next System* Project paper, available at: https://thenextsystem.org/rto#what-the-public-thinks

Gowan, P. and Viktorsson, M.T. (2017) Revisiting the Meidner Plan. *Jacobin*, available at: https://www.jacobinmag.com

Graham-McLay, C. (2018) A 4-day week? A test run shows a surprising result. *New York Times*, 19 July.

Guinan, J. (2019) Socialising capital: looking back on the

References

Meidner Plan. *International Journal of Public Policy*, 15 (1–2), 38–58.

Guinan, J. and O'Neill, M. (2019) From community wealth building to system change: local roots for economic transformation. *IPPR Progressive Review*, 25 (4), 382–92.

Gylfason, T. (2012) Iceland: direct democracy in action. *Open Democracy*, available at: https://www.opende mocracy.net/en/iceland-direct-democracy-in-action/

Gylfason, T. (2014) Constitution on ice. CESifo Working Paper Series No. 5056. Available at: https://ssrn.com/abstract=2529896

Harvey, D. (2003) *The New Imperialism*. Oxford: Oxford University Press.

Hay, C. and Payne, A. (2015) *Civic Capitalism*. Cambridge: Polity.

Heales, C., Hodgson, M. and Rich, H. (2017) *Humanity at Work: Mondragon. Social Innovation Ecosystem Case Study*. London: The Young Foundation.

Hobsbawm, E. (1964) *Labouring Men: Studies in the History of Labour*. London: Weidenfeld and Nicolson.

Holloway, J. (2010) *Crack Capitalism*. London: Pluto.

ILO (2015) *World Employment and Social Outlook*. Geneva: International Labour Office.

James, S. (2008) Is transformation possible? They say we can't, we say we must. *Off Our Backs*, 38, 40–3.

Kerevan, G. (2019) Boris, Brexit and the hedge funds.

References

Bella Caledonia, 11 July, available at: https://bella caledonia.org.uk/2019/07/11/boris-brexit-and-the-he dge-funds-part-1/

Kishimoto, S. and Petitjean, O. (eds) (2017) *Reclaiming Public Services: How Cities and Citizens Are Turning Back Privatisation*. Paris and Amsterdam: Transnational Institute.

Labour Party (2017) *Alternative models of ownership*. Report prepared for Shadow Cabinet, Labour Party, London.

Lapavitsas, C. (2013) *Profiting Without Producing: How Finance Exploits Us All*. London: Verso.

Lewis, J. (1992) Gender and the development of welfare regimes. *Journal of European Social Policy*, 2 (3), 159–73.

Luxemburg, R. (1968) *The Accumulation of Capital*. New York: Monthly Review Press.

MacKinnon, D. and Cumbers, A. (2019) *An Introduction to Economic Geography: Globalisation, Uneven Development and Place*, 3rd edn. Abingdon and New York: Routledge.

Malleson, T. (2013) Economic democracy: the left's big idea for the twenty-first century? *New Political Science*, 35, 84–108.

Mann, G. (2017) *In the Long Run We Are All Dead: Keynesianism, Political Economy and Revolution*. London: Verso.

Marois, T. (2017) *How Public Banks Can Help Finance*

References

a Green and Just Energy Transformation. Amsterdam: Transnational Institute.

Marx, K. and Engels, F. (1848) *Manifesto of the Communist Party*. Available at: https://www.marxists.org/archive/marx/works/download/pdf/Manifesto.pdf

Megill, A. (2002) *Karl Marx: The Burden of Reason (Why Marx Rejected Politics and the Market)*. Lanham, MD: Rowman and Littlefield.

Meidner, R. (1993) Why did the Swedish model fail? *Socialist Register*, 29, 211–28.

Menser, M. (2018) *We Decide! Theories and Cases in Participatory Democracy*. Philadelphia, PA: Temple University Press.

Minns, R. (1996) The social ownership of capital. *New Left Review*, I/219, 42–61.

Moody, K. (2018) *On New Terrain: How Capital is Reshaping the Battleground of Class War*. New York: Haymarket.

Morris, D. and Shapiro, I. (1993) *John Dewey: The Political Writings*. Minneapolis, MN: Hackett.

Mouffe, C. (2000) *Deliberative Democracy or Agonistic Pluralism*. Vienna: Institute for Advanced Studies.

Mouffe, C. (2005) *On the Political*. London: Routledge.

Müller-Jentsch, W. (2018) Seven decades of industrial relations in Germany: stability and change through joint learning processes. *Employee Relations*, 40 (4), 634–53.

References

Nadeau, C.A. and Glasmeier, A. (2019) New data up: calculation of the living wage. Available at: http://livingwage.mit.edu/articles/37-new-data-up-calculation-of-the-living-wage

Neurath, O. (1945) Physicalism, planning and the social sciences: bricks prepared for a discussion v. Hayek. *Otto Neurath Nachlass in Haarlem* 202 K.56, 26 July.

Nove, A. (1983) *The Economics of Feasible Socialism*. London: Allen and Unwin.

OECD (2015) *In It Together: Why Less Inequality Benefits All*. Paris: Organisation for Economic Cooperation and Development.

Office for National Statistics (2016) *Ownership of UK Quoted Shares: 2016*. Newport: ONS.

O'Neill, M. (2008) Three Rawlsian routes towards economic democracy. *Revue de Philosophie Économique*, 9 (1), 29–55.

Patel, R. and Gibbon, K. (2017) *Citizens, Participation and the Economy. Interim Report of the Citizens' Economic Council*. London: RSA.

Pateman, C. (1970) *Participation and Democratic Theory*. Cambridge: Cambridge University Press.

Pateman, C. (2012) Participatory democracy revisited. *Perspectives on Politics*, 10 (1), 7–19.

Peck, J. (2001) *Workfare States*. London: Guilford.

Phillips, L. (2016) *A Global Post-Democratic Order*. Amsterdam: Transnational Institute.

References

Piketty, T. and Saez, E. (2014) Inequality in the long run. *Science*, 344 (6186), 838–43.

Pontusson, J. (1984) Behind and beyond social democracy in Sweden. *New Left Review*, 69, 69–97.

Ramsay, M. (2005) A modest proposal: the case for a maximum wage. *Contemporary Politics*, 11, 201–16.

Rancière, J. (2001) Ten theses on politics. *Theory & Event*, 5 (3). Available at: www/journals/theory_and_event/v005/5.3ranciere.htm

Saville, R. (1993) Commanding heights. In J. Fyrth (ed.), *Labour's High Noon: The Government and the Economy 1945–51*. London: Lawrence and Wishart.

Sayer, A. (2014) *Why We Can't Afford the Rich*. Cambridge: Polity.

Schweickart, D. (2002) *After Capitalism*. New York: Rowan and Littlefield.

Smith, A. (2014) *Socially Useful Production*. STEPS Working Paper 58. Brighton: STEPS Centre.

Soerensen, H.C., Hansen, L.K., Hammarlund, K. and Larsen, J.H. (2003) *Experience with and Strategies for Public Involvement in Offshore Wind Projects*. Seminar on National Planning Procedures for Offshore Wind Energy in the EU, Institute for Infrastructure, Environment and Innovation, Brussels, Belgium, 5 June.

Solimano, A. (2014) *Economic Elites, Crises, and Democracy: Alternatives Beyond Neoliberal Capitalism*. Oxford: Oxford University Press.

References

Standing, G. (2011) *The Precariat: The New Dangerous Class*. London: Bloomsbury.

TCOTC (2014) *Eighth Report on the Convention on the Constitution: Economic, Social and Cultural Rights*. Dublin: The Convention on the Constitution.

Touchton, M. and Wampler, B. (2014) Improving social well-being through new democratic institutions. *Comparative Political Studies*, 47, 1442–69.

UN (1948) *Universal Declaration of Human Rights*. New York: United Nations.

Wainwright, H. (2003) *Reclaim the State: Experiments in Popular Democracy*. London: Verso.

Wainwright, H. (2018) *A New Politics from the Left*. Cambridge: Polity.

Wainwright, H. and Holloway, J. (2011) Crack capitalism or reclaim the State. Red Pepper, 15 April. Available at: https://www.redpepper.org.uk/crack-capitalism-or-reclaim-the-state/

Weitbrecht, H. and Müller-Jentsch, W. (eds) (2003) *The Changing Contours of German Industrial Relations*. Munich: Rainer Hampp.

Widerquist, K. (2018) *A Critical Analysis of Basic Income Experiments for Researchers, Policymakers, and Citizens*. Cham, Switzerland: Springer Nature.

World Bank (2003) Participatory approaches in budgeting and public expenditure management. *Word Bank Social Development Notes*, 71.

Wright, E.O. (2001) Working-class power, capitalist-class

References

interests, and class compromise. *American Journal of Sociology*, 105 (4), 957–1002.

Wright, E.O. (2011) *Envisioning Real Utopias*. London: Verso.

Zamagni, S. and Zamagni, V. (2011) *Cooperative Enterprise: Facing the Challenge of Globalisation*. Cheltenham: Edward Elgar.